tricks with trees

tricks with trees

ivan hicks and richard rosenfeld

photography by jo whitworth

PAVILION

ACKNOWLEDGEMENTS

IH: To Angie, Stuart, Kama, Alice, Lydia and Miles
RR: To Elizabeth, Alex, Nora and Anne
and to our agent, Charles, for his *Guinness Book of Records* patience

First published in the United Kingdom in 2007 by
Pavilion Books
10 Southcombe Street
London
W14 0RA

An imprint of Anova Books Company Ltd

Design and layout © Pavilion, 2007
Text © Richard Rosenfeld and Ivan Hicks, 2007
Photography © see picture credits

The moral right of the authors has been asserted.

Senior Editor: Emily Preece-Morrison
Designer: Louise Leffler at Sticks Design
Picture Researchers: Emily Hedges and David Penrose
Photographer: Jo Whitworth, unless otherwise credited (*see page 160*)
Copy Editor: Annelise Evans
Indexer: Richard Rosenfeld

ISBN 9781862057340

A CIP catalogue record for this book is available from the British Library.

2 4 6 8 10 9 7 5 3 1

Reproduction by Mission Productions, Hong Kong
Printed and bound by C T Printing, China

www.anovabooks.com

CONTENTS

INTRODUCTION

MANIPULATION OR MUTILATION?

This book tackles everything from the super-pristine to the completely bonkers. Trees jump out of the Platonic ideal category and become a kind of Playdo: with a spadeful of pluck and know-how you can turn them into knots and quadrupeds, cheesegraters and towers. If it sounds new, or an iconoclastic/*faux-naif* attempt to break out of mainstream gardening, it isn't. It's just that everyone's been miles away, arms crossed and humming, on a spiritual-cultural shelf.

Thomas Pakenham groups his ancient, whopping trees, capable of eliciting a "Wow", under headings like "Grizzlies", "Gods" and "Ghosts". His trees have Personality. Sacramental dignity. They're historically alive. They verge on what R.S. Thomas called "the miracle of the lit bush". Simon Schama called tree groves a "fitting décor for our earthly remains", a kind of rearing up, tangled headstone. To neo-Romantics, trees fling you to extremes, to ecstasy or terror. To the nostalgic, they're *the* ingredients to a vital, mythic, private, pastoral landscape. Goethe linked Gothic cathedral columns and the sublime beauty of trees to God, as if every trunk contained a "Hold tight" rocket lift to Heaven, and that was without seeing Gaudi's whacky great cathedral, the *Sagrada Familia* in Barcelona, which he began in 1884 and is

still a building site inside. But what's missing? Trees as growing, expanding sculptures: as beds, bumps and balls.

Pack saplings close together, 30cm (1ft) apart in a semi-circle, then prune and re-route their growth and you've got a gallimaufry of shapes: cafés, igloos and twisters. Plant 12–20 *leylandii* in a circle 3–4m (10–13ft) wide, remove the inner branches, let the trunks shoot up, add wooden floors and you've got a space rocket/tower. What follows (from page 24) are suggestions, not equations set in concrete.

Extreme tree shaping (like the granny knot, page 65) usually gets a "HowtheheckdidtheydoTHAT?", followed by a screeching "Not in MY backyard". And in some gardens, it'd be crackers, even if you had time to build an armature then train, tweak and pray. Fair enough. But you can't be sniffy and say "It's not proper gardening" because most of the following tricks come straight from the mainstream past. What gets our goat is this squawking squiffy obsession with topiarized box balls and spirals. And nothing else. Like the incredible emphasis on those piled up, fat little pug-eyed concrete frogs in garden centres given a revolting splatter of paint.

But back to tree shaping and Ivan Hicks. How did he get started?

I spent all my time bunking off school in the 1950s and '60s, climbing into these great big ruined Victorian houses in London with completely overgrown gardens, packed with trees and climbers. When I was older, I'd go to the Tate Gallery in my lunch hour, straight to the surrealists. I'd practically be the only one there. And gradually the two influences – the strange trees and extraordinary, bizarre paintings – came together.

I loved trees, studied arboriculture and knew trees inside out. Then I met Edward James [the whimsical, irascible, millionaire patron of Salvador Dali and René Magritte, with homes at West Dean in Sussex, in France, Ireland and Italy] when he was 64, and I went round the world with him as head-gardener, bag-handler and companion. He had 2,000 acres in Mexico where he had been making amazing architectural follies in the jungle, painted reds and blues and golds, covered in butterflies as big as a fist. Then we'd go and create a large formal garden in Italy. He let me develop my style.

All of which lead to Ivan's 0.5 acre (0.2 ha) walled "Garden In Mind" in West Sussex, started with £500 in 1991 to create a surreal garden in five months for television. It was the only thing of its kind in the UK ("was", not "is", because it was bulldozed to make room for a garden centre in 2002

and Sir Roy Strong slammed those responsible in *The Times*). It had 1.2m (4ft) long metal tear drops dangling in trees, bendy bridges made from bent-over saplings, a typewriter barnacled with sedums, mirrors zinging sun glare, great flapping *Paulownia* leaves thwacking you in the face, arches made out of *Ginkgo biloba*s above a path of metal discs like armadillos set in concrete. On BBC's *Gardener's World* he threw a conifer over a hedge, and after more high jinx a gardening big-wig at Hampton Court shouted at him, "I condemn you out of hand."

So this isn't the kind of brain-emptying sycophantic gardening you get in the glossies, where everything is exquisite with a "must-see", "splash" "riot of colour", when anyone can see it's the horticultural equivalent of Habitat. This book veers between gardening for traditionalists – lovers of topiarized bumps and tunnels and arbours – and gardening for mavericks, daring fascists who understand that gardening means absolute control, who love trees and know how they grow, who can almost see right through the bark and all those jammed-together-reinforcing "drinking straws", and who secretly love that gulping look in a visitor's eyeballs when they step into the garden and see a fizzing porcupine of white birches, and "Why the heck didn't I think of *that?*" is glottal-veined on the forehead.

Right: Ivan Hicks' "Lewis Carroll Clock Tree". Stand beneath it to remember things that are just about to happen.

chapter 1

HOW TREES GRO

We were going to stick the theory right at the back before the index – even *inside* the index – so that the book didn't turn into a techno-manual, but decided that a few principles of tree growth would illuminate everything which follows. So here it is. The tree guide…

The trunk is an incredibly smart engineering feat. It's a bendy, armoured pillar-cum-two-way-feeding-mechanism which holds up a gigantic self-feeding photosynthetic factory, weighing over a ton, to the light. It doesn't shoot up from the base like a telescope (the first fallacy). The branches are fixed at the same height for ever and ever, and it's the tips of the tree that extend. And when a tree drinks up water and minerals, piping them round the system, it doesn't (the second fallacy) pump them up. They get hauled and sucked up from the top of the tree – that's 112.7m (369¾ft) high in the case of the tallest redwood – by incredible tension. Mature oaks can drag up over 500 litres (110 gallons) a day to replace that lost largely through transpiration (evaporation via the leaves). The columns of water get pulled to the top and, in extreme cases, they've been clocked doing over 35m (115ft) per hour.

Now the autopsy (facing page). The protective outer **bark** is a thick, corky, waterproof, shock-absorbing, fire-protective skin that's made of air-filled cells, which also helps regulate the inner temperature in extreme conditions. In the case of the redwoods it can be 1.2m (6ft) thick, although the trees ignite OK in an inferno. The soft, non-woody stems of a perennial die down each year, but a tree can survive without doing that; it doesn't need to keep starting from scratch.

Some bark is armed with toxins, resins, or latex and so on, to fight off bark-boring insects and fungal diseases, and some bark is a terrific cure-all. Bark from the South American cinchona tree (*Cinchona officinalis*) doesn't just gum

Above: Weight lifting. One of a trunk's key aims is to hold up the foliage to the sun for maximum photosynthesis.
Facing page: A cross-section of a trunk. Trees annually create new rings on every woody part – the anchoring, feeding roots, the twigs, branches and trunk. They can reduce the area that needs covering by bark only by dropping the twigs and branches. Pollarding and coppicing also reduces the amount of bark covering, with the result that trees live longer. If a tree's growth rate is held back or reduced, death is delayed.

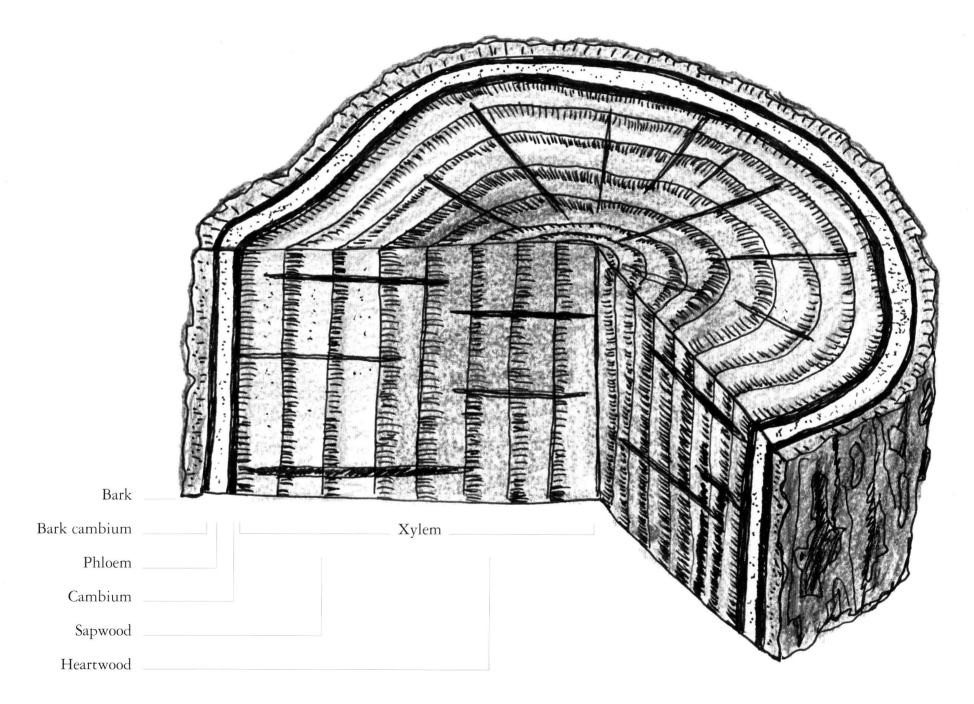

Bark

Bark cambium

Phloem

Xylem

Cambium

Sapwood

Heartwood

up the mouths of insects, it once provided anti-malarial quinine, the white willow provided high quantities of salicylic acid and packets of aspirin, and the Indian neem tree (*Azadirachta indica*) is the best chemical factory you'll find – a potential male contraceptive, teeth cleaner and tonic, tackling everything from insects to fungi.

The bark protects and covers the soft, spongy **phloem** or feeding channel. It's a thin section of live tissue through which the sap and sugars head down from the leaves to the roots, feeding the rest of the tree. Right behind that is the even thinner - just one cell wide - highly active, slimy **cambium**. Its cells keep dividing, creating new phloem on one side and woody **xylem** on the inner side, where you get the annual growth rings as a tree gets fatter. It's actually growing a whole new outer skin, then another, one on top of the other.

The live, outer part of the xylem is the **sapwood**, the tree's other main feeding passage, through which water and minerals charge up from the roots. The inner, central part – the tree's core, the darker **heartwood** which is packed with resins and tannins – is the older, dead bit, the absolutely essential pillar giving extra structural support. (Vicious mediaeval English longbows, used to slaughter the French at Agincourt, were made from yew strips incorporating both tough heartwood and the incredibly springy, flexible sapwood, but they weren't top of the range because Spanish yew was even better.)

A tree's feeding ability, its massive distribution network, bendiness and strength – wood is about a hundred times more robust than say fibreglass, still making it the best material for trees just in case you thought the synthetics or petrochemical industry had come up with something even better – owes its success to one dominating, repeating feature. The majority of reinforced cells make microscopically thin, vertical, hollow tubes, and they're

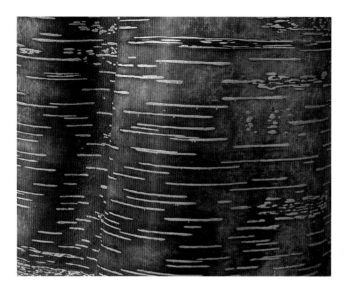

Facing page: Roots like three elongated, headless, flat-bellied gods perched on the ruins, their feet touching the ground.
Above: The blistered-looking horizontal lenticels, or raised pores, on a birch. They enable gases, especially oxygen, to penetrate to underlying, live tissues and can create extraordinary, distinguishing marks. Look for the diamond-shaped lenticels on poplars, especially *Populus simonii*.

tightly rammed together, running up the length of the tapering trunk, giving extra strength. The design couldn't be bettered, and completely relies on a stiffening, anti-buckling agent – the chemical lignin – which radically toughens the cellulose cells. Cellulose minus lignin is totally non-erect and floppy; the trees would go kaput and collapse. With it, you get vertical, rock-hard wood. (The most abundant organic materials on Earth are cellulose in first place, with lignin in second, and if you disagree email *Encyclopaedia Britannica*.) It's quite a surprise, then, after all that hydraulics and structural engineering, when you look at a tree, say a Samuel Palmer-like *In a Shoreham Garden* apple tree, blobbed with bloom and fizzing with energy, to hear that four-fifths of its cells are dead. Only one-fifth of a tree is alive.

GROWTH RATE AND LIGHT

Crudely, trees grow in stages. They're competitively fast when young, slow up in middle age, add a few centimetres a year as OAPs and then, depending on the species, tick over in senescence, shedding unnecessary limbs and the inner heartwood. Some tree boffins argue that mature trees don't need the heart-wood, and that if it rots the tree becomes hollow and loses weight, making it less likely to go flying in a gale.

The key factor affecting a tree's growth and shape, besides water and minerals, is the availability of light. All the extension growth is locked in the tips of the shoots, which contain the crucial apical cells. These leading or dominant buds are programmed to grow up to the light (called phototropism) and against gravity (geotropism). You can easily test that absolute need by laying a pot plant on the ground in summer. Its tip will quickly make an upward, right-angled flip. Now stand the pot up and this new growth will stay arthritically locked at a right angle, but the subsequent extension growth will again aim up for the light. Vertical, horizontal, vertical.

Above: The bizarre, wiggly branch of a beech tree (out of shot, to the left) aiming for the light. It has been forced down, by competition, but tenaciously loops off for the light. **Facing page:** Provided about one-fifth of the roots of a tree that has been blown down are still in the ground it should still do very well. Amazingly, tree roots don't grow deep, with 90cm (3ft) being about the maximum depth, with most not hitting even 30cm (1ft). The reserve buds on this flattened woodland tree have launched a row of replacement shoots. The tree won't keep growing horizontally, but will die back at its tip.

Trees with light and without it are completely different animals. As Colin Tudge says in *The Secret Life of Trees*, "Trees grown in open spaces may spread themselves like a Persian cat on a feather bed, and take on all manner of wondrous forms." Generally, a single parkland oak will develop a full, rounded, cabbage-like head of foliage and branches. It'll be squat and low-branched, perhaps with a thick, twisted trunk. But grow the same tree in a forest where it's fighting for light and it'll lose its lower branches and stretch up to the sun becoming taller, straighter and thinner, and it'll certainly be less sturdy because it won't have been given a good wind-shake (see page 136). This is one of the main principles of forestry. Plant trees close together in regimental rows to grow straight, with few lower branches and minimum knots in the timber. When they get taller, they're thinned. The weak are eliminated and the rest are left to grow thicker. The result? Uniform trees and a profit.

The trees in some of the following projects are grown incredibly close together, even centimetres apart. Does it matter? No. Two or more trees growing very close function as one tree, occupying the same space, and their crowns combine. Trees in groups, avenues and rows do exactly the same. But note that the closer they are, the longer it takes them to become as thick as a single tree because their crown and leaf area has been scrunched up and reduced. A wood can be seen as one tree with a whacking great big canopy and multiple stems. And if you think that's complicated…

EXTENDING TREE SHAPES

There are basically two types of broadleaf tree. The first group has a leading apical dominance (e.g. ash, lime, cherry and poplar), usually with a straight or forked (bifurcated) trunk. The second has a broad apical dominance (Japanese maple and oak) with a multi-branched head and often shorter trunk. The big distinction is that the first group is generally taller. Take two

Facing page: An avenue of beech trees, showing that they can be packed incredibly close together provided they're getting plenty of side light.

Above: No competition, no shade, and the luxury of a rounded head of foliage and branches.

examples: the tallest ashes in the UK reached 45m (150ft), although they are now restricted to 30m (100ft) high because of ash dieback, whereas the tallest UK Japanese maples hit 16m (53ft). The ashes are nearly three times taller.

Conifers – two paragraphs to go - are botanically simpler (their internal structure is less complex and they largely grow with one central axis) and older, having evolved millions of years before the broadleaves. They don't have reserve buds so they can't (with a few exceptions) be coppiced.

THE BUDS

A tree's branching style is immediately apparent in its arrangement of buds on a twig. They might be opposite (acer), alternate (beech) or randomly spiralling and clustered at the tip (oak). Compare mature, deciduous trees in winter and you'll see how each arrangement gives such trees their characteristic branching shape, and how it affects the crown. An English oak (*Quercus robur*) has clusters of small buds at each twig end, but they are frequently eaten by insects and birds. This means that one of the surviving buds to the side takes over, becoming the dominant extension, probably growing out at an angle, and because this keeps happening the oak gets its characteristic, angular zig-zag look. Ash trees are different because they generally have one fat black bud at each twig end, then two smaller ones behind to either side, usually resulting in a sinuous, single or bifurcated trunk. If the main bud gets eaten or fails, the two behind take over, and that's how it gets a Y shape.

Now the key bit. Most trees also have a reserve supply of latent or dormant buds, embedded in the bark. If damage, and that includes pruning, occurs higher up, they're activated and shoot out to replace the broken branch. While trees lose this self-healing, quick-fix ability as the wood gets older, many species are able, even when OAPs, to perpetuate themselves thanks to regrowth buds at the base when they are cut down or coppiced. But this doesn't apply to "tree ferns". They've no reserves, just one bud at the tip, so if one gets killed by the cold or eaten by mice, chuck it out. The same goes for conifers, barring a few exceptions e.g. the coastal redwood (*Sequoia sempervirens*), monkey puzzle (*Araucaria araucaria*) and yew (*Taxus baccata* – alright, it's not a true conifer), hence all those irrevocably bald, brown, gappy bits you end up with when you hack into the old wood in a cypress hedge, thinking it'll regrow. It won't. Don't do it.

THE END

All of which ultimately comes down to one point. Trees respond to natural calamities by activating their reserve buds. A tree KO'd by a gale, or partially uprooted, will respond by initiating these buds into upward-growing shoots. Bend a stem and you get the same result. The sap flow is restricted and chemicals accumulate, triggering dormant buds. Hence all those fruit trees with bent-over, flexible young stems, barnacled with stonking great thickets of fruit.

Facing page: An oak's highly distinctive, zig-zagging pattern of branches.

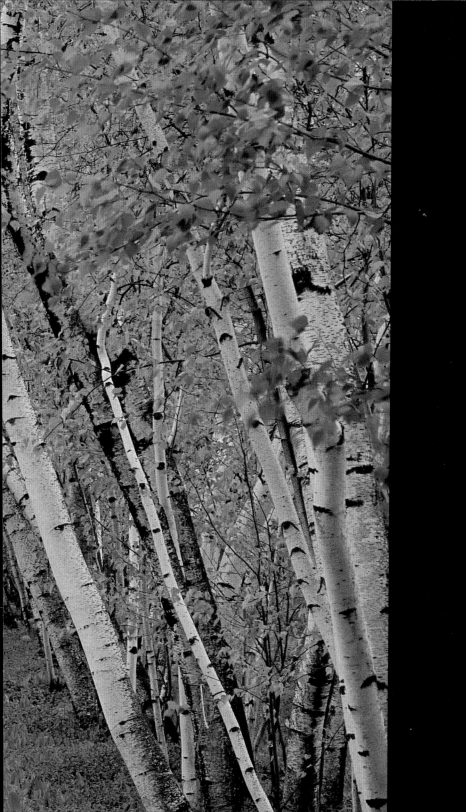

chapter 2

UPRIGHTS
AND TOW

ARCHES

An arch (see right) made from repeat plantings of hazel (*Corylus avellana*), which thrives on chalk. The hazels are set 1.8m (6ft) apart, and the bent-over growth has been bundled and tied together. As new shoots fire up from the base, and from the arched growth, tie them around the main stems, thickening up the arch.

The hazel's response to all this bending is to throw out new vertical growth on top, but you've got to keep nipping it back or it'll ruin the shape. If you don't check it, you'll get a tall sail of top-growth that'll get smacked around in a gale. Channel the sap where you want it to go, around the arc and not vertically on top of it. The bonus of hazel is the catkin show at the end of winter.

The plan is incredibly flexible, and you can amend it to create an igloo-cum-teepee like the one on page 56. Or plant the hazels close together and grow a tunnel. Or create a row of adjoining tunnels, so you're faced with – say – three entrances, running to different parts of the garden.

Previous spread: A tunnel of close-packed, angled silver birches.
Above: A Gothic arch of two birches (*Betula utilis* var. *jacquemontii*) with a vertical.

Facing page: Bare coppiced hazel in a woodland. By cutting back the growth to near ground level when it gets too tangled, you can start again with new shoots firing up from the base.

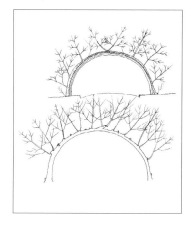

A bluish-grey arch (*facing page*) grown from two Atlas cedars (*Cedrus atlantica*). How? You'll need an armature made from an old polytunnel hoop, with one cedar planted at each foot. Keep strapping the trees to the hoop as they grow, but the key, which needs shouting out, is "shorten the sideshoots so they don't take over, but never completely slice them off." They'll help feed and strengthen the arch, and that has got to end up a tough, beefy, self-supporting structure because the metal hoop eventually gets thrown away.

Make sure that the growth at the bottom isn't shaded because the cedar needs light all over, and weave the ends of the two trees together when they meet, finally nipping off the tops. When the arch is self-supporting, you can either leave short growth poking out all round the trunk, or cut it off on the sides and bottom, so you've got a striking, bluish top fringe.

The ancient maidenhair tree (*Ginkgo biloba*), with leathery leaves like a duck's feet and fruit (on females) that reeks, also makes a nifty arch (*top left*). Young trees are incredibly rubbery and pliable, and they're grown like the cedars. At the back of the picture there's a ginkgo biped, with two trees angled at about 70 degrees, like a young Eiffel Tower or splayed giraffe. You can just grow a basic triangle and nip off the ends where they join, or let them shoot up. Again, the aim is to get thick, strong growth. And if you're good at this malarkey, try growing a huge round head, and two arms. A giant in the sky.

The two artworks are for a dayglo autumn arch. Use a red maple (*Acer rubrum*) on acid ground because the leaves, come autumn, look like they've been given a high-voltage scarlet zap.

Facing page: The basic up-and-over cedar arch from Ivan Hicks' "Garden in Mind", since pulverized and bulldozed, where he also grew a four-legged version. It had two plants on each side angled in, meeting above the centre of the path.
Top: Multi-purpose Chinese ginkgos. Relics from about 200 million years ago, they're incredibly good at withstanding the toxic worst of modern cities. Hardy ginkgos came to the West via Japan, the first UK tree being raised in 1754.
Above: The "Before" and "After" look of an acer arch. The top one shows the supporting armature, the bottom arch is thicker and self-supporting. And yes, the side growth is getting too long.

Above: A double row of five trees (use limes, rowans, birches, sorbus, etc.), the slight narrowing of the vista giving the optical illusion of extra length. The effect can be increased by using the tallest trees in the foreground and the midgets in the background.

Right: Giant poplars, close planted. You've got to know what you're in for. Hugh Johnson called them "an architectural incident".

AVENUES

Tree avenues divide into the immensely grand – with poplars (*middle left*), horse chestnuts (*Aesculus hippocastanum*) and sequoias, etc. – and the tiddlier domestic kind. Where to begin? Try small-leaved limes.

Tilia cordata is the nearest thing to an indestructible come-and-coppice-again tree. 'Swedish Upright' makes a tall, thin shape with spreading branches, and in midsummer it's thick with back-of-the-nose scented flowers that'll have you swiping away the bees. It's unbeatable planted in rows. The Mexican pine (*Pinus patula*), traditionally grown as a stand-alone, can be planted at 2.4m (8ft) intervals, and lightly pruned to create a flattish, tactile plane, with the branches linking, the grassy leaves dangling, and the tops stopped at about head height.

For an avenue-cum-hedge, grow tall, semi-naked beech. Keep shearing the leaves off one side (preferably the outer) so you're faced with a python of fat, bare stems. Leave a 15cm (6in) thin layer of leaves on top, and down the other side, giving the thinnest curtain of foliage that'll filter the light. The wider the avenue, the better, so that all sides get some sun.

Start by letting the beech reach it's final height, say 3m (10ft), then prune the top-growth in late autumn or early winter, as sap levels fall. At the same time, sheer the growth off one side. Old established hedges can be pruned over 2–3 years, to minimize the shock. And keep the bald side *bald*.

Above: An avenue of pyrus, that'll eventually form a tunnel, with the underplanting crying out for a flamethrower.

ARBOURS

Called "herbers" in the lingo of the Middle Ages, arbours can be circular, square, or rectangles-cum-tunnels with leafy walls, roofs and windows. The circular kind (*facing page*) is made with eight whitebeams (*Sorbus aria*), set about 2.4m (8ft) apart.

Use four old polytunnel hoops (or get a blacksmith to make them), and cross them over each other in the centre. Then plant a tree at each base. Leave the lower side-growth on, but keep it short, and strip it off when the eight tops meet in the centre. Leave the sideshoots on the top third though: they'll shoot out prolifically to create the roof, but keep them short or they'll soar away and take over. Whenever you grow in multiples, one tree is bound to be a runt, so grow one or two as reserves. Treat them like children with plenty of TLC, and bark ring anything taking off like a pheasant. Just cut out a narrow band of bark on a trunk, using a sharp knife, to arrest growth.

Alternatively, try evergreens in a semi-circle (*right*), with each tree growing up a tall post. Fix a cross beam to link the tops of the two end posts, with additional, shorter ones running from the cross beam to the tops of the other posts, creating a framework roof on which to train the topgrowth. Good trees include the fast-growing, shaggy Japanese cedar (*Cryptomeria japonica* Elegans Group) that veers between summer green and winter bronze. The semi-ever-green large shrub or small tree *Cotoneaster frigidus* 'Cornubia' forms a dome of arching branches with white, summer flowers, and is later massively barna-cled with red fruit. *Pyrus salicifolia* 'Pendula' has thickets of thin, bendy, weeping branches with white, spring flowers and striking, silver-grey leaves. Top choice, though, is the weeping aspen (*Populus tremula* 'Pendula'): a leaf-screen that quivers in the wheeziest breeze. Beware: it suckers prolifically.

Above: Five laburnums planted with a semi-circular hedge of golden yew. Plant all simultaneously, and keep the hedge at a sheltering shoulder height.

Facing page: A clever, eight-legged arbour and the even rarer sight of eight trees (whitebeams) growing at the *same* rate, with the *same* circumference. Don't count on it.

TOWERS

Forget the word "tower" and think of a very tall, circular hedge. Rapunzel's Tower (*left*) comes straight out of Grimm's fable – about obsessive-compulsive disorder with child stealing, hairy rope ladders and teenage single mothers in tower blocks – grown from a ring of Western red cedars (*Thuja plicata*). It'll take about 10 years to get one like this, about 3m (10ft) high.

Plant 20 trees in a circle, about 45cm (18in) apart. If you're doing it properly, grow the cedars on a raised mound simply because it looks smarter, with steps up to the front door. The wider the circle, the better, because more light gets to the centre. Use the stronger, thicker young trees on the shadier side, and the weaker ones on the sunnier side to avoid a big growth disparity.

As the trees grow, plait their branches: pull two together and wind them around each other. Create a cylinder of branches, trunks and clipped foliage, cutting off any shoots that ruin the shape. You could erect zip-up scaffolding inside to support the floors made from planks. Then add leaded windows, pointy Gothic doors and a ship's bell (better than a door knocker). You can leave the floor as grass, or spade it off, put down weed-supressant sheets, and cover that with gravel. The ultimate height depends on whether you're a scaredy pants, i.e. how high you'll go on a platform with a hedge trimmer. It could easily top 10m (33ft).

This page: "Before" – seven telegraph poles to bolster a circle of 30 fastigiate hornbeams, *Carpinus betulus* 'Frans Fontaine', that'll be planted with Virginia creepers giving a crackling red autumn zazz. The more basic tight circle of Western red cedars (*Thuja plicata)* has an inbuilt gap for the front door (*above right*).

Facing page: And "After". Put skeletons in the windows and light them up at night.

TREE HOUSES

The first idea is the house-on-raised-stage kind (*right*). Use strong vertical supports, adding a strong floor or platform*, and fix a garden shed on top. Then add flashing electric lights, mini-bar and Playstation 3. Next plant a tree in each corner, or more if necessary, unless you can start against a mature one, and train the branches around the shed, removing any poking in the wrong direction. Get it completely cocooned. For a more upmarket version you'll need a long, rectangular platform with a Gothic "shed".

Select fast-growing trees like limes, massive willows with pliable branches for training as a balustrade, or laburnums for their splattering thickets of yellow flowers when summer starts. Even better, make an apple-and-pear house using fruit trees so you just dangle a hand out the window and pick. Or out-do Bosch who used a crouching man's hollowed-out, hairless shell of a body as a house in his *Garden of Earthly Delights* (*c.* 1470). You just need a giant pod.

Tree houses are now big business, and you can order anything from a customized New England mega shed to the kind of covered, treetop walkways made for ancient Japanese gardens that let you wallow in puffballs of blossom. If you want to go completely tropical, nail giant banana leaves across the roof.

* Get everything checked by a professional to ensure that the floor and supports can take the weight of the shed, etc.

Above: A raised shed on a platform – a smart version of a grain store on legs to stop rats getting in. The tree on the left is the "Now" stage, the tree on the right is 10 years in the future.

Facing page: Get planning permission first... From Louis Audot's 1819 *Treatise on the composition and ornament of gardens*. Did it *ever* get beyond the design stage?

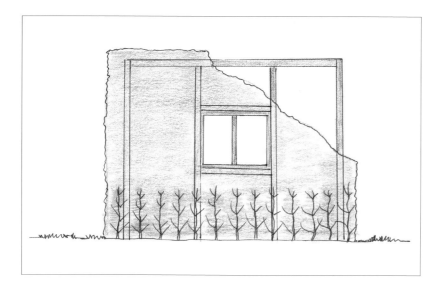

The big advantage of building a tree house** around a mature tree is that you get the trunk bursting out of the floor and spearing through the roof. The second idea, if you want to start at ground level, is to make a simple house from evergreen yews planted on a large square layout to make a giant, roofless Wendy house. Cut out (or add) doors, windows and a battlemented top. Or try four 10 x 10cm (4 x 4in) posts, each 2.4m (8ft) tall, in the corners of a square layout. Add a taller post in the centre and use lengths of taught, strong wire to devise a house with a high-pointed, sloping roof. Then plant four evergreen trees in the corners, and train the branches to the sides and up, pruning out any that grow in the wrong direction.

The third, instant option requires rough woodland and a close batch of saplings (*far left*). Weave lengths of willow around them, and that's the quick, desperate way for a "Keep out. GO AWAY. I'M NOT TALKING." box.

** As a rough guide, a load-bearing, strong, sound branch should be 20cm (8in) in diameter. Take professional advice, and check if you need planning consent.

Facing page: The ash tree house (designed by Ivan Hicks), at Groombridge Place in Kent. The wrap-round lengths of commercially available willow are easily bought from websites.

Top Left: The side-on plan for a basic, four-sided structure.
Below Left: First-storey circular tree houses topped by a penthouse, supported by trunks and poles.

TEMPLES

The quickest way to make a temple (*facing page*) is by planting a circle or semi-circle of spears, in this case white Himalayan birches (*Betula utilis* var. *jacquemontii*). Aim for a spare, striking, wide-spaced group and keep their stems clear (pruning off any side growth) for the first 3m (10ft), which is what professionals call "lifting the stems". Then let the crowns grow into each other.

Start with evenly sized maidens or short standards (see page 129), but note that the trees on the shady side won't grow as fast as those on the sunny side. Those falling behind need their sideshoots left on to help fuel more growth, while the taller ones need them stripping off to hold them back. It'll never work exactly; just don't get obsessive. A safe and sound green alternative is *Juniperus scopulorum* 'Skyrocket', a chopstick conifer; even at 2.4m (8ft) high it'll still be just 30cm (12in) wide, but note it'll be slightly thinner on shallow, quick-draining soil than on beefier, well-fed ground. Let it beanpole up.

Highlight the inner sanctuary by using fat, white pebbles on top of weed-suppressant matting, or try a whirlpool of children's marbles, sea shells or stained glass set in a pizza base of concrete. Buddhas are an upmarket option.

Facing page: Himalayan birches. Even if you don't want a temple, make the most of the white bark, packing them in flashy groups.

Far top left: A circle of snake-bark maples (acers), with linked, woven branches.
Above: A basic design using *Juniperus scopulorum* 'Skyrocket'.

Above left: A linked ring of oaks.
Above right: Silver birches with the flashy red growth of *Cornus alba* 'Sibirica'.

Facing page: To highlight the temple look, stand it on an island. The ring of birches alternates snappy white *Betula utilis* var. *jacquemontii* with the brown, pink and white bark of *Betula papyrifera* 'Vancouver', and the combined autumn leaf look is yellow and orange. Coppiced red dogwoods line the bank. The barely visible life-size sculpture in the middle is of Ivan in a bath with a butterfly on his toe and a frog on his knee.

TREE HENGES

A tree henge – a henge is a late Neolithic/early Bronze Age circular area, often ringed by a ditch and bank, possibly incorporating stone triliths – is a tree ring with attitude. With an enigmatic, weighty atmosphere.

This henge (*facing page*) has a double row of 80 oaks in a giant ring, with a pond in the middle. As the oaks grow, their branches spike each other's space, their trunks fatten and the path becomes increasingly thinner. The smallest possible single oak circle depends on how much sunny space you need in the centre, but a diameter of 5m (17ft) is fine. If you're still waiting to inherit a field, try the poplar ring (*near right*), which can have a minimum diameter of 2m (6½ft). Tweak the design by planting the poplars around the edge of a natural, circular hollow, even angling them in so that their heads eventually meet in the centre, where they sort themselves out and a great big head shoots up.

The hollow makes a good children's hideout, where they can be outrageously disgusting, with banks for rolling down and spaceships dangling from branches. Tie climbing ropes from opposite trunks, and goblinize the slopes by fixing old doors to the ground. For adults, try a downward-spiralling channel or rill of water, starting at the top of the mound and spinning round and round, with the water rushing out through a plug hole in the centre and being pumped back up, but get the leaves out quick. And to re-invent the stupendous, yellow-flowering laburnum arch, with rich purple, ball-headed alliums poking-out-of-the-ground idea (made famous by Rosemary Verey), plant up *Laburnum* x *watereri* 'Vossii' with the likes of *Allium aflatunense*, *A.* x *hollandicum* or *A.* 'Purple Sensation' right in the centre. It's still magic.

Facing page: In time, this will become a rustling, secluded space ringed by 80 oaks.
Above: Quick-sprinting Lombardy poplars (*Populus nigra* 'Italica') can hit 24m (80ft) in 30 years; larger specimens easily grow an extra 12m (40ft).

HAMMOCKS

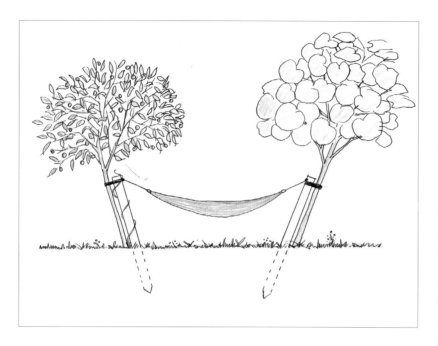

You don't need two trees for a hammock. Well not immediately. Thump two solid 15 x 15cm (6 x 6in) posts into the ground at a slight angle for attaching a hammock, and then plant the trees next to them, so that it eventually looks like the hammock is attached to the trunks. And you get the shade. (The trees won't continue growing at an angle because their heads quickly right themselves.)

Make sure that you plant good trees. Ornamental cherries give a great thwack of spring blossom, apples and pears thickets of fruit, and laburnums yellow flowers. If you are itchy-fingered, go for *Betula nigra* so that you can keep stripping off its bark. And sow grasses and wildflowers thickly all around to create an anti-thump butterfly and bee-buzzing mattress (*of course* you'll fall out).

Above left: Safe and simple, using angled trees and posts. To select the best tree, next time you're in an arboretum lie down under the likes of the Tibetan cherry (*Prunus serrula*) with its highly polished bark or the huge-leaved *Paulownia tomentosa*. See which scores best.

Facing page: Forget the posts if you've got a couple of power-house trees. Attaching the hammock with rope is the best bet – better than screwing in. Just make sure the trees widen towards the base so there's no slippage. Re-tie the rope every few years to avoid constriction.

CLOUD SEATS

There are two ways of making a high seat, basically a glorified stork's nest. Plant four trees with solid, horizontal, spreading branches on a 90cm (3ft) grid, and gradually snip out any shoots that grow in the wrong direction to give a solid, flattish spread. Cherry trees are top of the list, especially *Prunus* 'Shirotae', because of the way they grow, and because you can sleep entangled in blossom. The next step is making a wooden platform to strap to the branches, and hauling up a lilo.

Alternatively grow three *Salix alba* willows (e.g. the incredibly popular, quick-growing *S.* var. *vitellina* 'Britzensis') angled together, making a tripod. The tops should be just above the point where they intersect, at about 1.8m (6ft) high. Pollard them by cutting off the tops in late winter or early spring (then and only then). This forces out a furious batch of new growth from more or less the point where they intersect, and thickens and strengthens the trunks. Then up you climb.

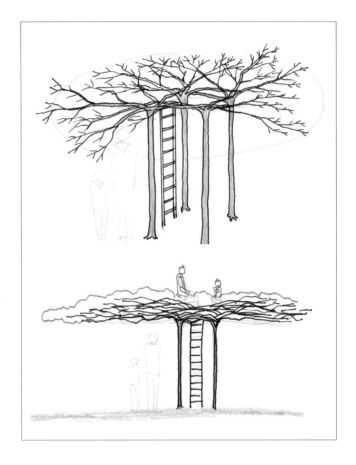

Above: Horizontal branching white cherries double as a bed or a child's anti-pirate, early-warning platform. To sleep in a tree, you just need a head for heights, a lilo, a safety harness and a hammer to whack in ear plugs against a bag-burst of shrieking egos (the dawn chorus).
Facing page: The Japanese *Prunus* 'Taihaku', which means "great, white cherry", makes an excellent cloud seat. One was sent to England long ago and completely forgotten about until Collingwood Ingram found it growing in Sussex, virtually dead but with one bough in full flower, and he identified it from an eighteenth-century Japanese print.

TREE BEDS

There are two ways of tackling the bed. Either use a wooden frame, like this one (*facing page*) made from eucalyptus, or make one using railway sleepers (*top left*) to create a rectangle. Fill the base with rubble and bricks to give good drainage, shovel on poor (not rich) garden soil, rake over and flatten, and then flick out anything (nails and flints) that'll prang you in the back. Now plant with creeping thymes, especially caraway thyme (*Thymus herba-barona*) which really does have a strong whiff of caraway, at gaps of 20cm (8in), and/or lawn chamomile (*Chamaemelum nobile* 'Treneague') at 15cm (6in) gaps. Let it get thick and tufty and spread.

As for the corner trees, the contorted willow (*Salix babylonica* var. *pekinensis* 'Tortuosa') shoots about like a firefly, or gorge on apple, pear and plum (with "Necks among the thousand leaves,/Tongues around the fruit.") Or use the flagpole cherry *Prunus* 'Amanogawa', all pink blossom in spring and green-yellow-red leaves in autumn. Alternatively, train two trees at each end, like laburnums, growing them into an arch.

The quick, no-tree alternative involves using vertical trellis panels on three sides, nailed to the bed, with the climber *Holboellia coriacea* shooting up and a trellis roof for extra spread and shade. In Howard Hodgkin's painting *In Raimund Stecker's Garden*, there's a bed in an arbour with a fire-bomb explosion of colour. That's the aim.

Both pages: A willow bed by Mick Ford in Ivan Hicks' garden, with 2 contorted willows at the head end. **Top left:** A bed made from railway sleepers. Get rid of any weeds to stop them growing up the sides.

If the bed is being put on a lawn, spade off the surface beneath and put down weed-suppressant matting, and then cover with gravel so that the surface of the stones is flush with the surrounding lawn.

chapter 3

WILLOW

WICKED WILLOW
DOS AND DON'TS

Willow grows incredibly quickly when coppiced, firing out long lengths of new stem. They can be cut away after the leaves have dropped and stuck in the soil, where they'll quickly root and grow. You can use rods up to 3.6m (12ft) long. Willow can't stop regenerating. That's a plus and a headache.

The British native, the crack willow (*Salix fragilis*) is a 25m (80ft) giant, often seen as a large, waterside tree, sometimes on its back, with its trunk wedged in the mud and rooting. Don't use it for the projects described here because it's too brittle; other kinds are more pliable. It propagates itself from cuttings of wind-snapped twigs that crack off, land in muddy ground and root. In fact tree stakes made from willow poles have taken root and grown beside the newly planted ornamental tree they're meant to be supporting and, bizarrely, even sawn-off rings of willow being used as stepping stones in a boggy area can root. It's horticultural Lego.

Back to the willow rods. To root them, make a trench of well-prepared soil in autumn or early spring with plenty of organic matter (manure and compost) forked in. That's vital if the ground is on the dry side. Fix weed-suppressant matting over the top, and cut slits in it for planting the willow. Then cut lengths of willow from the current year's growth into pieces approximately 25–50cm (10–20in) long. When cutting the bottom ends of the pieces, give them a sloping angle so that you'll know which end is which. Willow can grow at either end, but you'll get the best results inserting the bottom ends from one-half to two-thirds deep.

Right: In a dry season, water willow cuttings and when the sides start thickening with leaves, trim with shears. With most of the following projects, you might have to coppice the willow in late winter after a couple of years or it'll grow into an almighty thicket, like a bowl of last week's spaghetti. Then you've got to tie in the new growth. And beware: it's rampant.

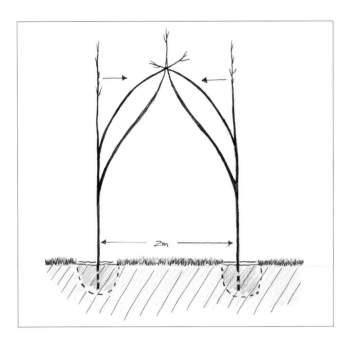

WILLOW ARCH/FENCE

If you've never tackled willow before, start with a willow fence. Choose either the high-powered *Salix viminalis*, which grows up to 4m (13ft) a year, or one with coloured stems. Set up supporting stout posts hammered into the ground every 1.8m (6ft), linked by horizontal lengths of taut wire. Then dig a 15cm (6in) wide trench along the base and get planting. Firmly wedge the willow rods in the ground, 20–30cm (8–12in) deep and 30cm (12in) apart. Aim for a criss-cross lattice, weaving them up, over and under. Loosely tie the rods to the wire to keep them in place, and nip off the growing points when they're about 1.8m (6ft) tall. Easy. So is a willow tunnel.

Mark out the sides of the tunnel and prepare two 30cm (12in) wide parallel trenches. Use 30cm (12in) long willow rods and firmly wedge them in the trenches, opposite each other. Tie them together in the centre when they meet. It's time-consuming and a pain in the back, so get help, and don't do it on a windy day. If you want a bit of oomph, put a focal point – a sculpture or fountain – at the end. You could even have four such tunnels, forming the four arms of a cross, with a private area right in the centre.

A charging-up-and-down snake tunnel for children could be long and straight, incredibly wiggly, circular, or a figure-of-eight, but check that it's wide enough for overtaking. Or make the tunnel an approach to a wigwam (*see over*).

Facing page: ... or try a mannequin, legs sticking up, out of the ground, balancing a disco ball or ice bucket. **Above:** Bending over lengths of willow to make an arch. All the sideshoots need cutting off, and every few years the plants need to be coppiced to create a fresh new structure.

WIGWAMS AND IGLOOS

With the photographer flat on his back, the igloo (*facing page*) looks gigantic, but it's not. The height is about 3m (9ft).

You'll need 50 or more long willow rods (*Salix viminalis*). Stick them in holes in the ground, made with a metal spike to speed things up, and set 30cm (2½ft) apart. Leave a gap for the doorway. When the rods are the right height, get help and stand someone on a chair in the centre. Tie the ends to a willow hoop to make the open top. If any rods die back, cut them hard back to 15cm (6in) above ground, and new shoots should appear. Prune to leave just one shoot, and that'll be the replacement. You can also weave long lengths horizontally around the structure, tied in with raffia, to re-inforce the shape and stability.

In the first year, new side growth will break out all over the stems. Some of it can be woven between the uprights, which is fine, but do not let the head get too big, bushy and top-heavy. Keep pruning. When the igloo eventually becomes chock-a-block with new growth, cut back all the stems in winter and start again.

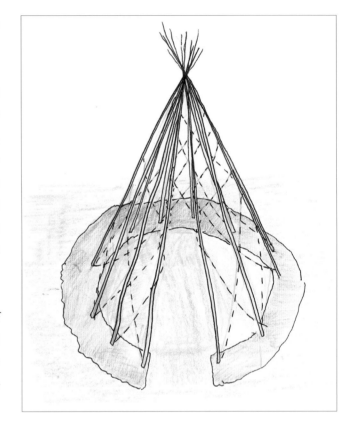

Above: The basic willow wigwam, with the stems pushed into the ground through weed-suppressant matting which covers a filled-in trench packed with manure and compost. Water well.
Facing page: A new igloo, all verticals, circles and squares.

WILLOW CHAIR

The chair (*near right*) has a couple of willow lengths planted against each leg, trained up and around, and copies the 1780–1830 Medieval Revival look, characterized by the pointy arch. It's based on the set of eight chairs commissioned by Horace Walpole for his home in Strawberry Hill, Twickenham, London. The simplest way to train the top-growth above the head is by tying it to long canes fixed by the two back legs. And if you want to be really ambitious, grow a long table and chairs.

The more basic version (*facing page*) is a simple wooden seat with coiled willow for the armrests, and a tangled flat plane for the back. Willow shoots are so pliable that you don't actually need a frame, but you can either make one out of canes or use an old, crude, basic chair, with or without the seat.

To make a fun pick-up-and-go chair, with stems that can be cut off at ground level, train new shoots from four plants – which will be firing out in all directions – to form the seat, and prune away the rest. In fact, keep pruning new growth all over to keep the shape. Gradually, the stems thicken and eventually you can cut through the base of the legs at ground level, pick it up and take it away. For a fixed, rooted-in-the-ground alternative, use lime or oak. And no, as the tree grows, the legs don't get longer and no, the seat won't suddenly be *up there*. The extension growth occurs at the top and the seat height stays the same. For ever.

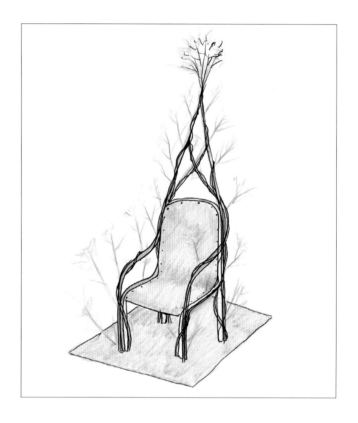

Above: Whatever happens, don't make an intricate plan with fiddly right angles because it's unrealizable.

Facing page: The early, tangled stages of a coiled willow chair needing some TLC.

WILLOWY IDEAS
BALLS, HARES AND INITIALS

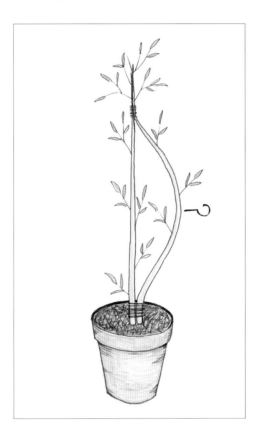

For a caged anything - blue ball, globe or lobster shell - start with one vertical willow cutting grown in the ground, and pollard it annually for say two years until the stem is thick and strong. The next spring, after pollarding, fix anything comic inside the cage of new growth, and tie the tops together, and then cut off the ends. Keep snipping off the leafy side growth. And the spring after that, you start again and pollard the top.

The cadaveric willow hare is big, about 2.4m (8ft) high, a bright idea if you want a Beatrix Potter take on the *Body Worlds* show of the German anatomist Gunther von Hagens. (He displayed the peeled, stripped-bare, preserved bodies of the dead using a technique called Plastination, the most in-your-face being a skinned man baring his skeletal muscles, blood vessels, and bones, riding a horse. Relatives are good alternatives.) Some of the hare's willow shoots are alive, rooted in the ground, and others are dead, attached to stakes in the ground that support the structure. The potential with willow is huge.

The idea for the willow hanger comes from Dr. Lois Walpole. Use two shoots, one for the vertical, one for the bow, and tie together at the top and bottom. Within two years the tissue will have fused together. The quickest way to fix the shape is by sticking a real coat hanger in the soil, and training the growth against it. Keep wet all summer, remove any sideshoots, and after cutting off at soil level attach the hook. New growth quickly shoots out of the plant in the pot. Use it. Grow a back scratcher. A cage for a cockatoo. You name it.

For those with spare land and names made from angular letters, plant willow stems in the ground to spell out a name. You don't need a template.

Facing page, left: A taut, clenched willow cage with blue ball. Even better, try a plastic lobster (*see page 1*).
Facing page, right: Revenge of the Giant Bunny (made by Kim Cresswell). Fix a hosepipe in its mouth, wait for a smarty pants child and...
Above: Growing your own coat hanger. It can be cut off at soil level and used.

chapter 4

MORE TRICKS WITH TREES

TREE TRAINING
A GRANNY KNOT

Trees are incredibly pliable. You can use acacia, figs, willow, even lime against a solid DIY frame – and that's absolutely essential – for training the trunks until they're "fixed". They're programmed to hit the vertical and will eventually (and you can just see this in the photograph, *facing page*) curve back to make an upright. But note, you'll need to keep the head in scale to the knotted legs or it'll bulge into a great big canopy. With the first gale the knot will go arse-up.

An easier alternative, especially if you think the knot is the equivalent of tree GBH, is growing two trees side-by-side, with just one "twist" above head height, giving an arch, and letting the trunks straighten immediately above it. Use plane trees and, where the trunks cross and touch, they'll inosculate or self-graft, giving some stability. But don't forget: the height of the arch will stay the same. There's no point making it 1.2m (4ft) above ground hoping one day it'll be twice that – it won't.

Victorian intricacy is a thousand times fiddlier (the two illustrations, *right*). Once you've plotted the pruning cuts on the design – forcing out new shoots to support the letter A, etc. – it's obvious how it works. We did commission an artwork and positioned a million pruning cuts but a) it's just a tangled mayhem of squiggly red lines and b) who the heck's going to make it? But one letter on a stand is, in theory, dead easy.

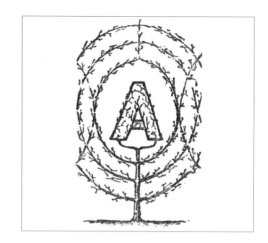

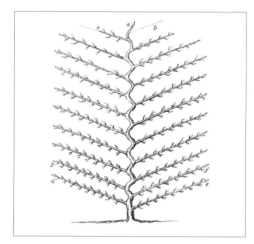

Facing page: The quotidian and the comic.
Top: Victorian tree writing. Use apples or pears on dwarf rootstock.

Above: An espalier for a pear tree with a "side-winder" vertical. The art is getting the arms to grow from the tip of each bulge without any hiccups.

TREE TRAINING "CHEESE GRATER"

The outrageous, stupendous Heath Robinson *Cheese Grater* by Axel Erlandson (our title, not his) using American sycamores (*Platanus occidentalis*). It looks complicated, but it isn't.

To create something similar, plant about six young London plane trees in a circle, and stop each leading stem to force out two new sideshoots from below, giving a Y shape. These new shoots are then trained up at 45 degrees, weaving them over and under. You'll need one mighty elaborate armature to keep a symmetrical shape. Where the criss-crossing shoots overlap and touch each other they'll eventually inosculate because, as said, plane trees self-graft, though pros like Erlandson would graft them together by removing a thin section of bark on both "arms", tying them together, letting the tissue fuse. The big problem is doing a Tarzan and climbing up to strip off the side growth. If you can crack that, you can finally stop weaving and let four "trunks" erupt from the head. Eventually, years ahead, the lattice growth will fatten and merge.

Above: Axel Erlandson's mammoth six-legged lattice tree with a perforated chest, four necks and leafy head which looks quite capable of waddling away.
Facing page: Axel Erlandson's version in an earlier, still thickening-up state.

MOON TREE

The aim is to create a small circle about 45cm (18in) wide on top of the nipped-back, vertical stem of a pliable lime, maple or white poplar (*Populus alba*). Left alone, it'll make a giant of a robust, suckering, quick-growing, slender tree, and when the leaves get blown about you get a fun, bi-coloured mix of the pale grey-green (on the top side) and silvery (below). It can be cut back to keep it shrubby, or try a moon tree instead.

Nip out the tip of the stem when 60–90cm (2–3ft) high in the spring, which will make it throw out new shoots at the top. Select the two strongest, remove the rest, and grow them around a bicycle wheel that has been firmly attached to a supporting tree stake. When these two shoots meet at the top, cross them over, taking one up to the left and one to the right. From now on you've got to cut back these two shoots poking up above the circle, each or every other spring, so that they stay about 15cm (6in) clear of the moon. And remove any other shoots the moment they appear or the tree will put up a hell of a fight to impose its natural shape. After about five years the two moon branches will be sturdy and you can throw away the wheel. (*See page 70* for step-by-step illustrations.)

It helps, when looking through the moon, to have a feature lined up in its sights. Or tie a disco ball (*see page 2*), coloured prism or piece of stained glass to hang inside. Alternatively grow a wide circle of moon poplars with anything in the middle from a Beckham wedding throne to a metal pyramid.

Above: A cartoon face in Ivan Hicks' "Garden In Mind". It was trained around a wheel, but in theory you could train any number of shoots around an object, and later remove it.
Facing page: If you want a wonky look, train shapes without a template. Painting is tackled on page 76.

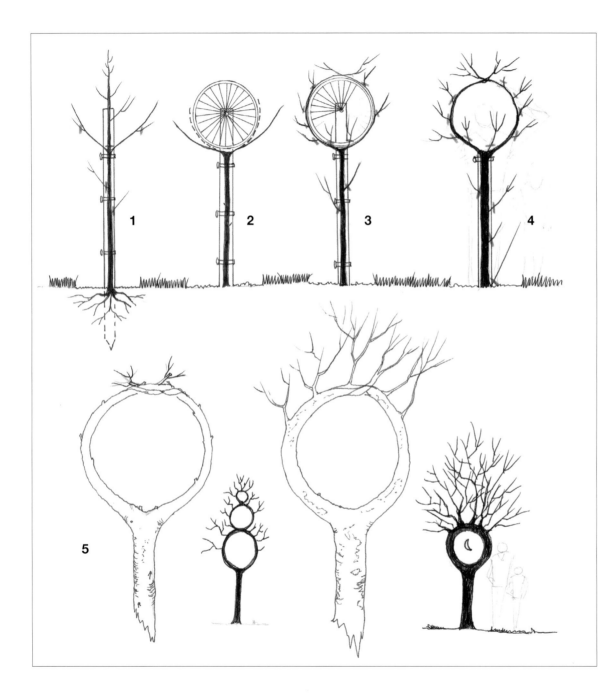

1 On planting, insert a post in the ground. Then remove the side growth, except for a strong pair of arms at the right height. Remove the central stem that was growing above that.

2 Attach the wheel to the post, with the bottom rim just above the pruned vertical stem.

3 Train the arms around the wheel, and remove any side growth.

4 Continue removing side growth.

5 The range of possible head shapes.

Facing page: Hazel man. With deft twiddling and pruning, you can create ears and hair; add sunglasses, bow tie and Panama hat.

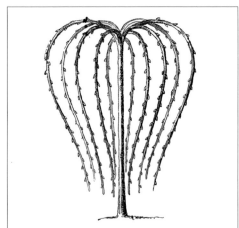

Left: The see-through apple globe.
Top: The cup is basically a circular, multi-stemmed cordon, with each arm being grown up a vertical metal stake. Depending on how fiddly you want to be, you can grow upward-angled side arms. Attach short lengths of wire, from stake to stake, for training them along.

Above: 'Fiesta' makes a good weeper because it has a naturally weeping shape, and a heavy crop of apples that taste like a Cox being crunchy, acid and juicy. Use MM11 rootstock which gives up to 3.7m (12ft) of growth, and stop it at say 2.1m (7ft) high. Keep nipping off any top growth which tries to ruin the shape.

Above: Plant two spur-bearing apple trees, angled in at say 70 degrees, each with a supporting stake, and where the trees touch, strap together. They'll then grow vertically, for which you'll probably need a tall, third, temporary stake.

Nip out one of the verticals half-way up the torso, using the strongest shoots below to make the horizontal arms. Train the other vertical straight up, and make a simple head by nipping off the stem top. Use the two strongest shoots below the cut to curve around a wheel making the face. Bingo. Apple man.

Keep pruning for shape. In late summer cut back sideshoots to 5-8cm (2-3in) above the base cluster of leaves.

APPLE GLOBE

Apple trees are regularly trained as step-overs, standards and half-standards, as pyramids and mini pyramids, and as cordons, espaliers and fans. Here are cups, weepers and globes.

For a globe (*facing page*) you'll need an apple tree on dwarfing rootstock (the rootstock determines vigour and height). M27 grows from 1.2–1.8m (4–6ft) high, M9 from 1.8–2.4m (6–8ft), and M26 from 2.4–3m (8–10ft) high, and your best bet is M26 because M27 and even 9 can be pretty weedy. Choose a spur-bearing tree (with fruit on the sideshoots along the main branches) and not the tip-bearing kind (fruit at the tip of a shoot), and buy it as a maiden. It'll crop a year after it has been stopped, and you can eventually expect about 4.5kg (10lb) of fruit a year.

Grow in a sheltered hotspot, make sure that the soil is deep and rich with good drainage (not thin and poor), and keep grass and weeds well away. Before planting insert a permanent, vertical metal stake (with M27, 9, and 26 it'll need to be permanent because the root systems aren't that strong), and weld an open, four-armed ball frame on top bought from a topiary nursery, or get one specially made. Train the leading stem up to say 1.5m (5ft) high, just above the base of the ball. After it has been stopped or nipped out in winter, the top four new shoots that break out should roughly correspond to the base of the metal ball. Well that's the aim. (Get rid of any others.) Train each one up and over to the top, tying them in with raffia. When the four arms meet, nip off the ends. Because the arms have been curved, plenty of buds (that'll become fruiting sideshoots) will appear, and they need to be pruned back to three buds from the main arm in late summer. Good alternatives are the cup and weeper (*see left*).

FRAMING WITH HAWTHORNS

Semi-abandoned "installations" can be given the chunky treatment using huge blocks of oak, squared off (*top right*), or a stump on its head (*facing page*). The latter is framed by seven *Crataegus tanacetifolia* that'll gradually fatten and fill the gaps between the roots.

Why *C. tanacetifolia*? It's a good, tough, slow-growing hawthorn. It does a midsummer fling with scented white flowers, and has orange-yellow round fruit that stands out against the grey-green leaves, and best of all it's thornless. There's no training: just plant and go. The heads merge into one canopy, with no thinning necessary. Plant small trees about the same size and, if one races away, lop off a main branch or two and that'll reduce its leafy self-feeding, self-energizing growth rate. And where do you get gigantic old tree stumps? Try specialist stump-removers on the internet, or tree surgeons, agricultural colleges and gamekeepers.

If you want to be slightly flashier, go for a tree with coloured bark. Top choices include the silver, and green striped snakebark maples (*see pages 140–1*), birches with white, orange and copper/pinkish bark, eucalyptuses – especially the amazing snow gum (*Eucalyptus pauciflora* subsp. *niphophila*) and urn gum (*E. urnigera*), peeling stewartias, (go straight for *Stewartia pseudocamellia* Koreana Group), Persian ironwood (*Parrotia persica*), and the highly strokable, peelable *Prunus serrula* with shiny brown bark. The ball (*bottom right*) is hemmed in by birches.

Facing page above: A new Ivan Hicks design in Dorset with uniform, well-behaved hawthorns. No runts, no sprinters.

Right: The cubic tree seat, part of the same design, using four Washington thorns (*Crataegus phaeneopyrum*).

Facing page below: Birch and stone ball. Use a wide, rough, chunky ball forcing the lower trunks out, making them grow up and around the ball, hemming it in place.

TREE WRAPPING AND PAINTING

Start with a dead tree, but it has got to have smooth bark, like beech. That's essential. It has also got to have a few shapely, thick, angular branches, but if it is chock-a-block with growth saw off all the extraneous branches and shoots because (a) it has got to look smart and spare, and (b) you've got to paint it. You can also use a live tree, but people get ridiculously squeamish and think they're going to kill it, but that won't happen if they use water-based paint because it will allow the tree to breathe. And it won't wash off.

As for colour schemes …. Try dull (not screaming) yellow-orange, mimicking bamboos like *Phyllostachys bambusoides* 'Castillonis' and 'Holochrysa', or broad diagonals in black and white, or paint three-quarters of the trunk rich green so it looks like the grass has scampered up. Better still, go completely OTT with fun red and blue stripes – a Barcelona football shirt – and RONALDINHO down the middle. Also try powder-based paint, from children's shops, to spray the foliage and trunks and create a magic wood for a kids' party. The rain will wash it off.

There's nothing new in this. Magritte put imagery on tree trunks in his paintings, the ancient Persians sheathed trees in copper sheets and studded them with jewels, and the Mexicans whitewash trees. Why? To deter insects from shredding the leaves, and/or make them stand out so that birds can pick them off? Great fat juicy targets.

Right: Wrapping a tree in silver foil for a temporary art display. We've also seen dead trees sprayed with an adhesive, compost and grass seed that'll quickly germinate, bringing it to life for a year.

TREE DRESSING

Ignore the gardening chatter about vertical space "with dainty roses exploding out of the canopy" which makes you want to *****. (We wanted to use words like vo*it but the editor said, "Over my dead body.") Everyone's duped by the lingo completely forgetting that branches double as pegs for objects. For hanging up giant gongs, thongs, mirrors and even mannequin Eves dangling gigantic apples labelled "Take me". Paul Cooper woke everyone up in the mid-1990s with his sexy garden at the Chelsea Flower Show, with a "condom tree" right in the middle (he actually tied Typhoo tea bags to the branches). Anything goes. Try skips, builders' yards and car boot sales.

This spread, and pages 80–81: Three Ivan Hicks "installations" using cubes, clocks, wine bottles, mirrorballs and "wishes".

UNUSUAL IDEAS

Don't use plants like ducks on a wall. Copy Matisse. Use colour. Add jokes. Soak visitors. Italian Renaissance garden owners, for all that amazing high chic, could be just like Benny Hill. They used hidden water jets – *giochi d'aqua* (water jokes) – to squirt visiting dignitaries.

Here (*near right*), the top part of the tree doubles as a mast and lets children Captain Sparrow their way to the crow's nest. Surround it with gravel and black cardboard triangles stuck in the ground for shark's fins, and use an aspen because its leaves flutter in the twangiest breeze. You could also try a tree growing through an old car, a Fiat Fiasco, with a hole sawn out of the roof and floor.

The poplar (*centre*) has had its head cut off, with all the regrowth scrunched up. The pregnant stem (optional) is easily created by hammering a second stake into the ground close to the supporting one on planting, which lets you bend the growing tip towards it, then up, and back to the first stake. When the stem gets to about 1.5m (5ft) high, nip it back generating a ball of fuzz.

Tree lighting (*facing page*) generally gets the up- or down-lighting treatment with angled spotlights. This is magnificently OTT. Use great lengths of Christmas lights.

Above left: A beach garden, fronting a wide pond, with grasses and large pebbles tumbling into increasingly smaller ones. Extra likely plants include *Allium scorodoprasum*, buddleias, globe thistles (*Echinops bannaticus*), sea holly (*Eryngium maritimum*), sea kale (*Crambe maritima*), sedums and valerian (*Centranthus ruber*) for the authentic picture. If the stones are covering decent, rich garden soil anything goes providing there are more pebbles than plants, and the plants have a scrunched up, cabbagey look.
Above right: A poplar rictusing Edvard Munch's *Scream* (well almost), shock waves of primal fear exploding out of the mouth.
Facing page: Nothing succeeds like excess.

chapter 5

BALLS, BUMPS
AND BUNDLING

JAPANESE CLOUD PRUNING

Oriental cloud pruning means giving shrubs and conifers bare arms, topped by Brussels sprouts. The Holy of Holies is the Japanese holly (*Ilex crenata*) because it's hardy, evergreen, is happy in containers (highlighting the shape), produces long, leggy shoots when young and has small leaves which means you get chunky, rounded heads with leaves that don't get slashed when pruning. It hasn't been available that long in the West. It went from Japan to the czar's garden in St. Petersburg in 1864, and then to Europe, with more plants going straight to America around 1900 where it's now a big hit as a landscape shape, and there's intense work creating new hybrids.

Get a 90–120cm (3-4ft) high specimen, the nearer to the final height you want the better, and think Japanese. You've got to envisage its hidden, essential sculptural shape and strip away the clutter. Then get hacking, with plenty of pauses to step-back, sizing it up, being as arty as you can. Expose its "essence", keeping say three main strong stems with side branches, and cut off the extraneous growth. You can even shape the branches into arthritic old bendiness by getting a book on bonsai, and see how they wire up branches to give them a permanent twist.

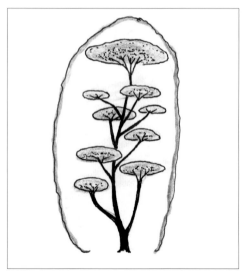

When it has grown to the right height, nip off the stem tips and strip off the leaves up most of the stems, pruning what's left into asymmetrical, wonky balls. The only potential problem with the blobs is that they umbrella or bounce off the rain, and the compost in a pot stays dry. Give it regular summer drinks and a spring feed with blood, fish and bone. Other likely conifers include the Japanese cedar (*Cryptomeria japonica*) and Japanese black pine (*Pinus thunbergii*), the Chinese privet (*Ligustrum delavayanum*) and leyland cypress (x *Cupressocyparis leylandii*).

Right: Not so much cloud pruning as a Mike Tyson octopus with boxing gloves, freshly aroused. The best way to avoid climbing up stonking great big trees for pruning is to cramp plants in containers. Given a limited root run, their growth potential is hugely reduced.

Facing page: Sculpting a blobby lump of growth, aiming for shapely branches with layered balls or discs.

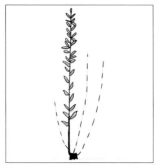

Left: A double row of holm oaks (*Quercus ilex*) upgraded to balls on 2.1m (7ft) high legs. The tricky bit is keeping them equal, the supererogatory, insane bit is castellating the edge of the lawn so that each trunk is precisely 'x' centimetres from the side edges, and *keeping* it that way.

Top: Coppice an existing evergreen shrub (e.g. bay), select the strongest shoot, cut out the others, and train as described.

Above: Upgrade a shrub by removing everything except for a sturdy, upright stem, then stop and strip it to create the bare leg topped by a ball.

MOP-HEADED TREES

Bolt upright lollipops or mop-heads, like these evergreen holm oaks (*Quercus ilex*, *facing page*), shriek out Renaissance formality. You can either buy a ready-made mop-head — nurseries are packed with outrageously priced potted bays and box snapped up by smart restaurants — or make your own. Get an evergreen with a single, sturdy stem (or with one strong stem, and weedier ones which you can cut off), but don't immediately turn it into a mini, junior lollipop and then try growing it bigger. Wait. It has got to reach the right height - most shrubs grow about 23cm (9in) a year — when you nip out the main or leading shoot in late spring or summer to force out plenty of new growth on top. Keep nipping it out to make the head extra bushy.

While the plant is growing taller, leave the side growth on because it has got a short-term use, feeding the plant, creating a thick, solid trunk. If this growth starts getting too long and becoming too dominant, then shorten it but don't eradicate entirely. Not yet. Wait until the head is getting bushy. Once the head is taking shape, start giving it a regular trim; use secateurs on large-leaved plants like bay so that you don't cut across and slash the leaves, and shears on small-leaved plants (like box) because that isn't a problem. *Lonicera nitida* 'Baggesen's Gold' is a good choice for a 90cm (3ft) high leg. Being floppy it needs staking but it shoots up fast and is extremely bushy, needing regular clipping. Golden privet (*Ligustrum ovalifolium* 'Aureum') also gets top marks.

If this sounds incredibly fiddly and precious, ignore everything we've said. Look for an overweight fatso shrub in the garden and get hacking, reducing it to a single, sturdy vertical stem, leaving a ball of green on top. Experts will squawk "Don't massacre it all in one go, go gently for a few weeks, adding an all-purpose feed," but if you're dying to attack, ATTACK. Likely contenders include young Japanese privet (*Ligustrum japonicum*), bay (*Laurus nobilis*), leyland cypress (x *Cupressocyparis leylandii*) or any cypress-like conifer with a vertical stem. You can either buy or make a (chicken) wire globe or cage (tightly binding two semi-spherical hanging baskets together), then temporarily secure it over the head and snip off any growth when it starts poking through. The moment the head makes a smart ball, get rid of the frame. Or "snort" down a Bloody Mary and tackle it freehand.

You can easily go one better if you find balls on legs absolutely, disgracefully twee. Create a Sputnik by leaving one strong shoot to poke out of the head each side, like Frankenstein's monster (not so much mixing as car-crashing metaphors), with an extra one on top, and let them grow a few inches. Then stop them to create a ball of green about the size of a grapefruit at the end of the shoot, stripping the leaves off the rest of it. You could go completely OTT by adding an old TV aerial but at that point, we say, Enough. (Also see coppicing, page 100.)

TOPIARY

First, the outrageous. Copy a painting. James Mason (the American teacher of sculpture, not the punctilious, throaty English actor who starred in *Fanny by Gaslight* and *Lolita*) topiarized Georges Seurat's 1886 *Sunday Afternoon on the Island of La Grande Jatte*. Why? Seurat emphasized poise and outline, featureless faces and stares. He refused to flatter reality. Mason couldn't wait to topiarize 54 people out of yew (*Taxus baccata*) - the tallest is 3.5m (11ft) high - and eight boats, dogs, a monkey and cat, all in 0.5 acres in the Topiary Park in Columbus, Ohio.

Or Google the Topiary Cemetery in Tulcan, Ecuador, 3,000m (9,840ft) above sea level, close to the Colombian border. An oneiric mix of South American imagery, Samuel Beckett and *Alice's Adventures in Wonderland*. The cuboid, wide-eyed faces – straight out of *Happy Days* – look like they've been buried right up to their jaw. It was created in 1936 by José María Azael Franco Guerrero using *Cupressus arizonica* after the town's first cemetery had been smashed by an earthquake.

If that's too much, get a 3D metal frame (stock Disney animal shapes are available from garden centres; better, design your own and contact a blacksmith), wrap chicken wire around it and stand over a box plant. Then snip off the growth when it pokes through. Or buy a bushy shrub and shape it freehand. Use small-leaved plants for shapes with precise, tight angles. Big favourites include box, yew and *Lonicera nitida*. If you're making a cube or trigonal trapezohedron, buy a 30cm (12in) high box cutting. Either shape it now, or grow it until it's bigger than the shape you want, giving regular trims to make it bushy. The same for spirals. They need to be 1m (3½ft) high before you start cutting them downwards. Walk around, size them up,

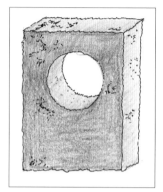 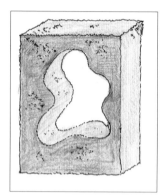

Above: Box or yew sculptures. Grow great slabs of foliage about 45cm (18in) thick, in a rectangle of bare soil in the centre of a lawn. Then shear off the sides, reducing the block to about 30cm (12in) wide, and cut out the holes. The bigger the slabs the better, and we mean 1.4–1.8m (4–6ft) high and wide. Don't try it on exposed sites because the wind will angle it over. In any event anchor it to four stakes in the ground, linked by walls of chicken wire, which will be hidden by the growth. Set the plants about 23cm (9in) apart.

Facing page: A zoo of metempsychosist figures and scalene-stomached dinosaurs.

and SNIP. Or spiral down a piece of rope, from toe to hem, and follow the line.

For a tree version, buy a conifer and train it up and around a pole, or grow the likes of a hornbeam (*Carpinus betulus*). Keep taking off new branches, and when it's 4m (13ft) high work up and around it with shears, turning it into a vertical, leafy corkscrew. Use yew for a 1.5m (5ft) high human because it grows quick and tall. If you can't do a freehand, intricate shape, grow box inside a frame. Again, stand it over the plant, and clip the growth as it pokes through. Trim all shapes in spring and summer.

That's the DIY side. In short, avoid anything that smacks of those revolting upright teddy bears perched on their bums like parrots. Try a "protoplasmal primordial atomic globule" (from *The Mikado*), and £100,000-a-week England players actually scoring penalties. Or (*right*), a wormhole, the theoretical hyperspace tunnel concocted by a couple of fizz-brained students for Carl Sagan's novel, *Contact*. The four bare-legged, mushroom-headed Portugal laurels (*Prunus lusitanica*), planted 60cm (2ft) apart (*right*), have a ladder tied to the branches with a tunnel "secateured" through the head.

Facing Page: A tactile, sculptural mound, set in a field of smaller replicas. Quoting "Like a flow of meanings with no speech" (Wallace Stevens) might help if point-scoring relatives quiz "Whatdoesitmean?"

Right: A quartet of Portugal laurels, heads like cored apples.

PLEACHING

Pleaching is the grand, formal way of highlighting and secluding an avenue by creating a raised, linear hedge about 1.5m (5ft) above ground, so that people can duck underneath, and get framed views between its legs. Or you can use it to screen a private space inside a bigger one.

To pleach, you've got a choice. Buy semi-trained trees or train them yourself but note, when positioning the trees, you need good ladder access to both sides for regular clipping. Limes are traditionally used but common hornbeam (*Carpinus betulus*) is best because it is tough with dense growth, has yellow-orange autumn colour and is marcescent (holding on to its withered leaves over winter). Its thin twigs are easily sheared, and it tends to leaf out in spring two weeks earlier than beech.

Hardly anyone uses the South American beech (*Nothofagus alpina*), but it makes a terrific screen with larger leaves like a hornbeam, blowtorching orange-red in autumn. Small-scale, badly ignored possibilities include long-life, non-suckering shrubs with long, bendy shoots like *Griselina littoralis*, and *Cotoneaster frigidus* 'Cornubia' packed with big red fruit.

The first point is that the trees are like great big sails and can easily get blown out of the ground when young, so deep staking – i.e. 90cm (3ft) in the ground – is absolutely vital, going as high as the top growth. You'll also need strong horizontal battens, canes or wires set about 60cm (2ft) apart for tying in and training the side branches until the growth is tough and solid. And the next bit reads like a DIY manual …

You need saplings with a strong, straight stem, setting them about 2.4–3m (8–10ft) apart, or closer if necessary. Tie in a sideshoot to each horizontal support (that's one shoot to the left and one to the right) as the vertical stem shoots up. Get rid of any others. Try and use shoots that are emerging from just below the side supports, so that they arch up to them, and do not bend down to them from above. Finally, once you've tied in the topmost shoot to one side, bend over the main stem to the other. Finito. Wait for the arms to join up and nip off the ends.

The next job is just like making a ground-level hedge thick and bushy. Keep nipping back the growth to create lots of sideshoots, and give a regular summer trim to keep the walls and the top - and don't forget that - straight and smooth. Advice? Hire a professional. Please … Have you ever sky-dived off a ladder with a hedge cutter ZZZZEEEOOOWing off your nose?

Top: Better than a dozen step-by-step photos, this shot shows the strong, vertical poles, nicely spaced side arms, and secure frame.
Right: An open, latticed look.

BUNDLING

"Bundling" was a Victorian term for close tree planting when they grew the likes of horse chestnuts so close together that the base of the trunks would merge to give a quick, solid, beefy look. It's exactly what happens when a squirrel hides a batch of seeds in the same whole, and they all shoot up. In fact you can grow 6-10 trees in the same hole and the trunks will eventually fuse. The smart bit is growing six different trees to see what'll happen, but they must have similar growth rates and heights. If that sounds too zany, try two different cherries or crab apples, like *Malus* x *robusta* 'Red Sentinel' and *M.* 'Butterball', giving fruit in bright red and yellow. Two trees in one.

The photographs (*facing page*) show the same willow, or willows – plural. Question. Does the photo, *near right*, show willow shoots planted around a tree? No. Twelve assorted willow shoots, from different species, were planted close together, being wrapped around each other as they shot up. They've grown together and *they* make the trunk. The growth woven around the outside are the new shoots firing up from the base. But use different coloured stems and, in the short term, it'll look amazing. Eventually the yellows, reds and greens darken, the variations go quiet, and the stems coalesce, but when they leaf out in spring you'll immediately spot what has happened. Some catkins will be silver, some yellow. And the leaves will be green and grey.

Other possibilities include two recent Ivan Hicks installations. Twenty-five oaks were planted in a circle, touching each other, so that you end up with the same kind of effect – but on a much wider scale – created by Axel Erlandson on page 66, but note that Axel's diamond gaps will eventually disappear. Ivan has also grown 12 coastal redwoods (*Sequoia sempervirens*) in a circle, about 1m (3½ft) wide, so that they eventually coalesce. He tied the side branches together to strengthen the shape, and left some branches growing across the central space to create rungs for climbing up, so that when it's fully grown you can have your photo taken, head grinning out the top.

Above: Willow wrapping. It's initially more fun using different coloured species, but the marzipan effect disappears as the growth gets thicker and older.

Just don't do a George Eastman. The inventor of the Kodak camera contemplated what he'd achieved, scribbled down, "My work is done. Why wait?" and blew his brains out.

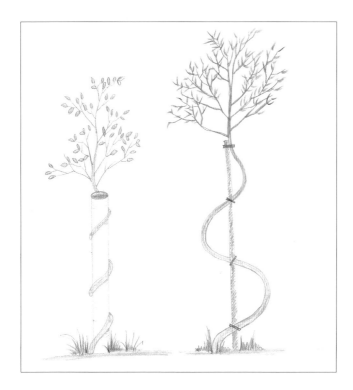

TWISTING

Garden centres are packed with mopheads on barley-sugar stems, trained around a thick cane, but you can go one better training one around a really wide length of pipe, seeing how it responds. Twisting is the next step.

The basic principle, and you can't get much simpler, is spelt out (*far left*), with a woodland goat willow (*Salix caprea*) – which produces staggering amounts of seed that get whipped up by the wind, which is why you get a cluster of trees on a distant scrap of land – trained around a swamp cypress (*Taxodium distichum*). You get a mix of upswept branches, fat, rounded growth, catkins and early spring flowers, *and* the taxodium's buttressed trunk (when grown by water) with autumn yellow leaves. Avoid the bizarre *S. c.* 'Kilmarnock' because it's a shortish, down-to-the-ground weeper, 2m (6ft) against 10m (30ft) high, and definitely not what you need.

The smaller photo (*centre*) shows what you can do with a duff old conifer. Prune its head into a giant oval, and then train a golden-stemmed willow up, round, and out. What you've got to do is pollard it high up each spring, forcing lashings of splayed shoots out of the head. In Ivan's word's, in winter it looks like an exploding egg.

Far left: A goat willow winding up a taxodium.
Centre: Just you wait. The conifer doesn't know what's about to hit it.
Above: Spirals and loops. Check that the spiral's cylinder is removed when the growth has become sturdy and fixed. To make the loop more elegant, grow another willow from the right, in the same way, creating a series of circles, decreasing in size, up the trunk.

COPPICING AND POLLARDING

The only difference between coppicing and pollarding (slicing off the top of a tree) is the height at which it's done. Coppicing, or stooling, is done from ground level to knee height, and most broadleaf trees quickly respond by firing out new replacement shoots, used for firewood, fencing, poles, you name it. Try it on the likes of a pine, and most other conifers, and you'll kill it.

To stop animals (rabbits, cattle and deer, etc.) from eating the spray of new, thin growth, coppicing was raised to head height, even to 4.5m (15ft) above ground, and became known as pollarding. The permanent trunk is a bolling. This cycle of cutting back was governed by the tree species, and the thickness of regrowth required. Willows, or withies, were cut back annually for their crop of thin, whippy shoots, but hazel, oak and ash were cut on 7–14 year cycles for thicker wood.

Now the rules. Regularly coppice trees in late winter or early spring, cutting or sawing back to leave a stump or stool about 30cm (12in) high. The cutting and regrowing of stumps increases their lifespan, with 2,000 year-old lime stumps having been found 16m (52ft) in diameter. Coppicing guarantees that the tree won't exceed its space and, in the case of the foxglove tree (*Paulownia tomentosa*), converts it into a flagpole. Reduced to just a couple of plump, fat shoots, all the tree's energy rushes into them, like lightning zapping Frankenstein's monster. They grow about 3m (9ft) high in one summer, producing leaves 75cm (30in) wide.

London planes and common limes respond extremely well, as do alder, ash, elm, willow, hornbeam and oak. The only time to pollard is again late winter or early spring because the trees then have high food reserves, and they'll have been well watered by the rain. Don't do it in autumn when the wood is dry, and don't do it in late spring because the tree will have already had its growth burst. If you must do it in summer, make sure that the tree is well watered in a drought. In the case of acers, stick to late winter to avoid any bleeding sap.

Also note, first, that young trees respond best, healing quickly and eliminating the risk of decay. Second, that you can't pollard most mature trees. And third, when you make next year's pollarding cut, you should make it just above the previous cut, sticking to new wood which, as said, is less likely to decay. Finally, once you've started the pollarding cycle, don't stop or the clattering poles will end up too solid and heavy for the trunk, and the tree will look like Edward Scissorhands on a mad hair day.

Right: The shaving brush effect of a pollarded tree.
Far Right: It doesn't look it, but the two sweet chestnuts (*Castanea sativa*) – untouched and coppiced – are about the same age. Coppicing prolongs the life of trees because they are constantly rejuvenating, "In effect, they step off the ladder of evolution ..." (Oliver Rackham, *Woodlands*). Some trees - hazels and coastal redwoods (*Sequoia sempervirens*) - even have a kind of inbuilt coppicing system, throwing up new shoots from the base if humans or animals don't intervene.

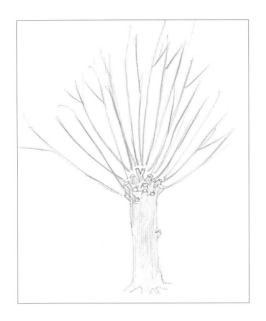

chapter 6

HEDGES AND EDGES

HEDGES

What's the point of a hedge? To slice up burglars – try getting through a berberis or pyracantha and tangling with 5cm (2in) long razor prongs – shelter wildlife, create vistas, or do clever, beautiful things? Get that clear and the rest is easy.

Informal hedges take no time. Farmers bung young, native, bare-root saplings around fields, slamming them in holes and then they're on their own. If you are after something much more arty, get sketching. Draw hedges in wavy lines creating mini compartments (see page 107), and play around with the tops – scalloping, castellating, and raising them step-by-step to a peak in the centre and down the other side. Or cut holes in hedges and insert stained glass and doors.

The ultimate wow of a hedge – and they're invariably magnificent accidents, like the one at Powis Castle, Wales – happened when gardeners were in short supply after World War One. Hedge-neglect created fantasy lumps on steroids (*far right*). The best way to get this effect, as designer Jacques Wirtz did on a smaller scale in his Belgium garden, is with an avenue of box, regularly trimming to make it bushy, then clipping in great sweeps to highlight an orgy of bottoms. Buy a variety of box plants with different shapes and heights. Then line them up to create a free-flow of organic shapes, and shear over to accentuate. Trim twice a year, in spring and late summer. Incidentally, the longest, cruellest hedge, if you want to break the record, was over 1,000 miles long and constituted a large part of the Customs Line in India, policed by 12,000 men. It consisted of thorny acacias and stretched, in 1869, from the foothills of the Himalayas nearly to the Bay of Bengal, to keep out vital supplies of cheap, smuggled salt.

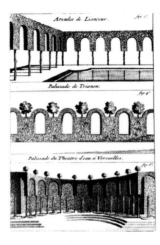

Above: Got a new hedge idea? Odds-on it has been done before, more stupendously, but you'll need obedient staff with a head for heights to beat these six plans.

Facing page: The yews (planted in the 1720s) at Powis Castle in Wales, all muscles, indents and pokings out.

UNDULATING AND WAVY HEDGES

Two contrasting hedging ideas. The angled-in wavy beech (*facing page*) must be mapped out using rope and pegs, marking out the lines so you can check they work, and a focal point – anything – is a must. You can upgrade the hedge by leaving entrance and exit gaps where the hedge swells out, and by planting two cherry trees at the end, on opposite sides. That's the easy bit. The arching-dipping box hedge (*left*) is trickier, but a good way of banding a garden, framing bowling alleys and borders. It'll only work if the hedging is kept sleek and low.

Excellent hedging plants include yew (absolutely unbeatable; initially slow growing but it quickly takes off), holly, hawthtorn, hornbeam and laurel. Privet is much maligned but a fantastic nectar plant that can be cut right back, and has rich green new leaves. Box is great for shorter height, but every time you open a gardening book it leaps out, so it's time to shout about yew.

Why *Taxus baccata*? It's tough, can be cut to the bone, regrows as high as you want, is dark green and makes a great backdrop for bright colours. But don't use yew in mazes where the bottoms get caught in the shade because they get horribly patchy and bare. When thinking about width, note that hedges ought to be slightly wider at the base than the top so all parts get good light, but plenty of stately grand hedges are absolutely upright and they look amazing. Cut for a crisp look in the first and second part of summer. Hedges are just like Lego. Have fun. Experiment. They are screaming out to be shaped.

Above: Let the box strips thicken up, then shear over, but keep running round the garden to check they work from every angle.
Facing page: In-out rows of beech, but check that close mowing won't be a nightmare. Most tree damage is caused by mowers and strimmers attempting to get a close cut.

DOOR AND WINDOWS

Hedging tricks kick off with doors and windows. You can start from scratch and wedge an old door or window frame tight against horizontal posts, and train a high hedge around it. And you can secure old bicycle wheels to make moon openings (*facing page*). But you can easily upgrade a mature hedge, cutting out such openings and jamming the frames and wheels in place. If you see a chucked-away old door with number, knocker and letterbox, grab it. Also look for old window frames and stained glass, even Venetian blinds.

It's insanely obvious, but check that a window frames a decent view. Gardening schools rattle on about the "borrowed landscape" when the suggestion is "Don't get a snapshot of a nuclear dump". It's worth studying the photographs in books on Chinese gardens. See how they insert the most exquisite, incredibly ornate wrought-iron window frames in a courtyard wall to frame a stylized tree or shrub on the other side that has been pared down to what they'd call its essential, elegant shape.

And don't stop there. Grow hedges to cut across paths and put an arch within. One way of adding to the impact of entering a terrific new garden area is by putting in a low roofed arch that forces you to bend right down, look down and up, reinforcing the surprise. Narnia fans need a wardrobe, packed with tatty old clothes to fight through, wedged in a hedge with an opening on the other side. But the other side needs a design that'll make your eyes pop.

Also try a heavy duty trellis with a screening of thick, woody climbers (e.g ivy or *Akebia quinata*, the climbing chocolate vine with small, dark purple spring flowers with a vanilla scent when the sun's out). Hardly a hedge, but no matter.

Above: A Gothic arch made out of four canes, or get a blacksmith to make the rods.
Facing page: A trellis with climbers and a framed view to bonsai-like trees. Make sure the trellis is a strapping heavyweight, fixed in place, if it's going to be head-butted by gales.

TAPESTRY HEDGES

You've got three options for an ornamental, mixed-ingredient hedge, (1) aristocratic, (2) Laura Ashley or (3) wild. The best ingredients for Option 3 include hawthorn with its vicious, skin-slashing thorny density, white spring flowers and nesting sites for blackbirds; field maple (*Acer campestre*), with *A.* 'Royal Ruby' giving new reddish-purple leaves; separate male and female hollies for red berries; and any of blackthorn (more birds), buckthorn (caterpillars), dogwood, oak and privet (berries). Avoid hazel and elder, a hedge's enemy, because they're impossible to constrain and will ruin the shape.

Plant at intervals of 25–45cm (10–18in) in a single straight row, one staggered row, or in two parallel, staggered rows for extra thickness. Use two-year-old plants, and cut off the top third making them shoot out dense growth at the base. Forest trees (e.g. oak, beech and hornbeam) are quite happy locked in twiggy dwarfdom. Let the growth intermingle to get a mix of leaf shapes and colours.

Option 2 means planting separate colours to let them merge, or keep them in separate cubes. Dark greens (box or yew), blackish-purple lightening to ginger in winter (copper beech), silvery green (elaeagnus), and yellow (golden privet) can be fun or a bit of a shocker, but if you leave wide gaps between the blocks, and link their tops by securely fixed metal hoops, and train top growth over them, creating arches, that's fine. Better still, go for a silver-black look with *Olearia* 'Henry Travers', whose leaves are grey-green on top and silvery below, or *Elaeagnus angustifolia* 'Quicksilver' which lives up to its name, alternated with a particularly blackish-copper beech (*Fagus sylvatica* Atropurpurea Group).

Option 1, going grand and stately, means using tall, well-heeled, well-clipped shapes and the subtlest of subtle variations in green, avoiding a marzipan shock. Check the combination works by comparing leaf colours in midsummer – before buying, in a garden centre – when they have lost their juvenile tones.

Right: A rare sight along a
tapestry hedge of coloured cubes.

LEYLAND CYPRESS

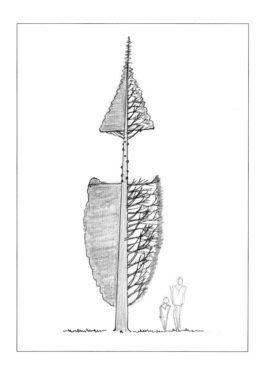

What's wrong with *leylandii?* Everything, when grown by a maniac. It grows at 1m (3½ft) a year for 20 years, then at 60cm (2ft) a year, and reaches two-thirds the height of Nelson's column which is 51.2m (168ft). When a hedge exceeds the height of a ladder (check, it could be illegal) and can't be clipped, that's it. You've got a Berlin Wall. But if you've got a spare field where it can't drive neighbours crackers, let one rip. And it's a terrific sight, a vigorous freak of a self-powering, pointy column.

Given its beanpole parents, the 30m (100ft) high North American *Chamaecyparis nootkatensis* – some are thousands of years old – and the 40m (130ft) high *Cupressus macrocarpa* which grows in just a few places in the Santa Cruz Mountains in California, it's no wonder that their sprog (x *Cupressocyparis leylandii*) fizzes up like a rocket. It was found at Leighton Hall in Wales in 1888, near its mum and dad, and its genetic instability means it has spawned plenty of variations like the bright yellow 'Golconda'. All make excellent hedges, but let it know who's boss.

A young hedge needs pruning twice in its first year, in mid-spring to get rid of long sideshoots and, in midsummer, for an overall trim. Keep trimming the sides (not the leading shoots) in the following years and, when it has reached the required height, nip back the leading shoots in mid-spring. Don't worry if it's now fractionally too low because the new growth will bring it back up to the required level. From now on, give the occasional all-over trim from spring to autumn. Overgrown hedges can be reduced by about one-third in mid-spring, but note that if you cut off the greenery and go into bare wood, that's what you'll be left with. Brown. It won't resprout.

Far left: A *leylandii* trained into an arch topped by a picture frame.
Above: Converting a fully grown *leylandii* into a platform and pod. You've got to got to climb up, pruning away the dead growth and thin twigs, using the branches as a ladder. Then cut away all the growth where you want the gap, hauling up a wooden platform that'll take your weight, fixing it to the trunk and horizontal branches on which it's resting. Note the top of the pod will keep growing. (Good insurance advisable.) It took the *leylandii* about 60 years before it became popular in the 1950s, since when sales have apparently topped 60 million.

chapter 7

HISTORY, FUTURE
AND GROWING TIPS

Topiary's first big burst runs from Pliny the Elder to the Eureka flash when it was rediscovered by Renaissance Italy. That's the official history. The ancient Persians clearly knew about hedge shaping, and that's a couple of hundred years before Pliny but don't ask for details, no one's got a clue. The Italians went completely OTT creating everything from box elephants and ships to popes and donkeys, mixing art, fun and satire. You'd have thought they'd have had a go pornography, as at Longleat in Wiltshire. There is an extremely fruity Sun Maze created by Randoll Coate. From the tourists' angle it's all extremely lofty, with classical images "drawn" by low hedging – the minotaur, Daedalus and Bacchus – but when the owner, Lord Bath, throws open his upstairs bedroom window first thing in the morning he isn't looking at Bacchus. No way. Those evergreen lines, the pictures, are wham-bang right out of the *Kama Sutra*. But back to the history. The Roman topia was an ornamental garden, and the topiarist a slave, and if you think you're a slave to your garden, think how they felt.

More slaves from more countries meant more ideas being imported to Rome, the Romans exported them with their empire, and so topiary-cum-formality took off. The French joined in. André Le Nôtre (1613–1700) redesigned the grand parterre at Fontainebleu and set about Vaux-le-Vicomte (his first great garden) which so rattled Louis XIV that he ordered Le Nôtre to make him an even bigger, better garden at Versailles. Flattening the ground and installing the roads, etc., took 30,000 men. All the outlandish topiary at Versailles (which even then was hard to find) has since been flattened and that's a double shame because, as everyone copies the past, they don't realize how buoyantly inventive it was. When Louis' son married in 1745, the king held a "Ball of the Clipped Yew Trees", an Elton-John-style fancy dress party, and turned up like a topiarized yew. So. Italy and France. Then Holland and Germany.

Previous spread: Place the bicycle in the crotch of a young tree, wedging it amongst the stems. The tissue grows over anything firmly fixed against it, and after 10 years it'll look like this. Because the tree's extension growth takes place at the top, the bike stays at the same height. The cheat's way is to nail up two halves of a bicycle.
Facing page: *La Complainte de Nature à l'Alchimiste Errant* (1516) by Jean Perréal showing real or imagined, highly intricate tree training.

And what happened in England? Landscaping. Well a chunk of park and lake might be thrilling in some sites, but at places like Petworth House in West Sussex, where the site is dwarfed by 60m (200ft) high chalk hills and fields, what's the point of a flat lump of lawn like a dead haddock? Nature – and you've only got to look up – has already gone one better. What did they think they were doing? If only the UK had been invaded (again) by Rome. Or Spain. Imagine Petworth now. Cake-stand fountains, grottoes, cascades. But topiary didn't die out. Elvaston Castle, in Derbyshire, in the mid-nineteenth century was the garden that relaunched topiary and garden "rooms". Because the owner, the Fourth Earl of Harrington, was a recluse hardly anyone saw what he'd done until his death, but when they did …

Eyes popped at the sight of 18km (11 miles) of bendy, slithering hedges periodically holed like a Swiss cheese with topiarized pepper pots and chopsticks of dark green yew, golden yew grafted on top, with minarets and mounds and igloos, a scattering of experimental ecstasy. It completely flouts everything in those shatteringly awful, constipated, garden design books. Apparently one gardener given a private tour couldn't believe it, and rolled on the ground kicking his heels in the air. Now it's a country park with nothing left.

Traditional topiary featured strongly at great gardens like Hidcote but, bizarrely, by the early 1980s you had problems buying topiarized box in the UK. It often had to be imported from Europe. Rosemary Verey brought it back into fashion, and specialist nurseries sprang up. (The first time Richard Rosenfeld met her, she was just opening up one morning and, not knowing who the hell he was, she snapped "Pick that up" – pointing at a hosepipe on the ground – "and put it over there". He couldn't believe his luck. He thought she was raving. Did he get that wrong.) Now the same shapes are

Facing page: John "Dammit it" Krubsack and his (once) living *Acer negundo* chair which he took on tour and which caught the eye of Mickey Mouse.

everywhere, but everyone is superglued to the same template, except for the likes of Jacques Wirtz. He leaps out because of his long rows of swooping, bulging, topiarized box that you only see on a bigger scale when a giant hedge has been ignored, turning into moundy, stacked-up tumps. Which brings us to the Gang of Four, and to an extraordinary offshoot of traditional topiary: training the likes of willow and trees into tripods and chairs and space rockets.

It hasn't got a name: Richard Reames calls it arborsculpture, which doesn't exactly fly out the mouth; TREEGOSHING (tree growing and shaping) might be better. It's hardly new, and there's a marvellous miniature, *La Complainte de Nature à l'Alchimiste Errant* (1516) by the poet-painter Jean Perréal (c. 1450–1530) – the most famous French artist of his time, astronomer, *valet de chambre* to three French kings, inspector of buildings and chief negotiator in the marriage between Louis XII and Mary Tudor, who was sent to England to check out her fashion sense – showing a seat formed from a growing tree. Its interwoven branches are trained and cross-grafted to form the seat and back, and the rather cross angel in the background looks like a highly unstable publisher who can't get anything right.

TREEGOSHING picks up in recent times with Arthur Wiechula (1868–1941); twinkly and bald-headed with a short, white pointy beard and John Lennon glasses. He was too ambitious. He was a German engineer and ecologist who wrote back-to-nature self-sufficiency books, and was influenced by Emanuel Swedenborg's vision of trees coerced into living houses, but few of Wiechula's ideas were realized; too impracticable, taking too long to finish. But what ideas. His plan for a huge, living barn is stupendous (*see opposite*). The outer walls are grown from three parallel, close-together rows of trees, and the growth goes straight up, then makes an upturned V-shape, then another beside it, and a third V, all forming the roof, and then down the other wall. Extra trees provide the internal supports, and the whole structure is about 12m (40ft) wide and deep.

John Krubsack (1858–1941) – 'Dammit it, one of these days I am going to grow a piece of furniture that will be better and stronger than any human hands can build' – was a Wisconsin banker-farmer and occasional furniture maker. He had, and we're guessing here, seen trees growing into fantastic shapes and then tried growing a tree chair about 1.8m (6ft) high when cut free. *The Chair That Grew*, as it became known, was sown in 1908 when he planted seed for 28 box elder trees (*Acer negundo*) to a plan that initially looked a right tangle, but he watched them – did he *study* them – watering and nurturing, until he could graft the trunks together to form the legs, seat, the back and the arms. He had some major panics when he thought one of the trees was dying but, with a prayer and a drink, they survived. In 1915 he took it on tour and, in 1988, Mickey Mouse sat on it on his sixtieth birthday. One funny idea on top of another.

Axel Erlandson (1884–1964) was a Californian bean farmer

Above right: Arthur Wiechula's
living barn.
Right: A smartly clipped
ficus house (see
arborsmith.com/world_tour.html).

At the Tree Circus near Santa Cruz, Calif.

Left: Art or revenge. A quadruped directly above its creator, Axel Erlandson, about to suck him up its trunk. It's amazingly easy to grow using a London or Oriental plane in the UK, where the American sycamore is a complete No-No. Or try lime or whitebeam.

Set four trees about 2.4m (8ft) apart, each one against the inward-facing part of a 2.7m (9ft) high, stout stake. You'll have to fix thin lengths of wood from the tops of the opposite stakes (forming an X shape if you're looking down on it from above). You'll also need one taller, central post when the stems come together and shoot up. Train the trees up the verticals, along the diagonal horizontals, then up the central post where they're tied together. They'll take a few years to inosculate (i.e. coalesce).

Above: Tree bending in John Claudius Loudon's 1838, eight-volume *Arboretum et Fruticetum Britannicum* (packed with 2,500 engravings). Why do it? So that when the tree – here a fast-growing common larch (*Larix decidua*) - is cut, you've got a one-piece prow for a ship. With the wood in one piece, it's inherently stronger than assembled pieces nailed together.

who pruned, shaped and grafted over 70 trees in 40 years, initially for fun. Hardly anyone knew what he was doing; when they did ask his secret they didn't get much more than "I talk to them." He grew a spiral staircase and telephone booth tree, and planted six sycamores in a circle, stopping them at 30cm (1ft) high, before grafting them together and creating diamond patterns (see pages 66-67) for the first 2.5m (8½ft). He also grew a nine-rung ladder tree (page 125) from box elder (*Acer negundo*). But if ever anyone needed a publicist … his family persuaded him to buy a piece of land on a tourist route in California, and he opened his Tree Circus in 1947. One child visitor was Richard Reames.

Reames is Erlandson's *alter ego*, and now the biggest American name in arborsculpture, who has gone public with slide shows, lecture tours, etc., (see his website, www.arborsmith.com). He grows just about anything, from tables and houses to rowing boats, and says fast-growing trees are good for practicing and learning. His mantra is "the right tree for the right place".

He began in 1992 with a living archway using close-planted hybrid poplars, and checked the growth of any quick sprinters that'd ruin the shape, outgrowing the rest, by bark ringing (cutting out a narrow band of bark on a trunk, using a sharp knife, to arrest growth). He's best known for his peace sign in the trunk of a cherry tree, a cube in a plum tree, and a circle in a magnolia. He also grows trees and chairs in pots, and cuts them off at the base, and then they're ready to use. Bigger projects include 77 flexible red alders (*Alnus rubra*) – which he likes for growing chairs – in a 6cm (20ft) diameter circle that'll become a giant cave-house. This isn't tricksy but eco-friendly, and if your eyebrows do a Lady Bracknell at the thought of a living house, then his fruit house – interweaving apple, pear and cherry trees eventually giving great thickets of fruit on the walls - sounds amazing.

Reames' favourite trees include alder, ash, sycamore, white birch, poplar, Japanese maple, cherry, apple, pear, eucalyptus, willow, oak and ponderosa pine (*Pinus ponderosa*), a timber tree in the USA. His enemies include stem rot, borer worms, aphids and deer. A quick interview with us went like this …

Q: "He's crackers thinking tree houses have a practical future?" That's what people will say.
A: *The fact is that trees can grow together. Trees can be grown into solid walls; it is only a matter of learning the proper techniques and developing ways to speed up the whole process. If enough people put their minds to the idea, we will be able to grow the living tree house, of this I am sure.*

Q: But what about creature comforts?
A: *The idea of growing a weather-tight structure is just too good to not give it a serious try. The ecological benefits are immense. All modern conveniences can be incorporated into the living house. Electrical wiring and plumbing is easily held inside the tree, and heating the interior is simple enough.*

Q: And what are your most popular commissions?
A: *Chairs and tables, benches and gazebos.*

Q: And the most unusual?
A: *The growing boat.*

But to the question, What would be the most amazing arborsculpture you could ever make? he refused to comment, saying that'd be too arrogant. Which is fair enough. Others worth checking out include Lois Walpole (www.loiswalpole.com), Dr. Chris Cattle, Dan Ladd (www.danladd.com) and especially the extraordinary www.pooktre.com.

Right: Richard Reames' living, fattening, growing boat, an extraordinary, elaborate lashing together of the pragmatic and fantastic.

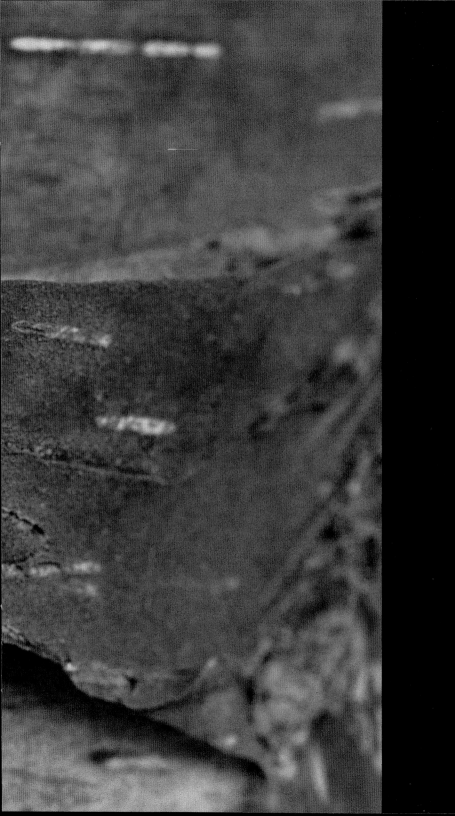

chapter 8

BUYING A
PLANTING

You can track down trees — even the incredibly rare — in seconds. The annually updated *RHS Plant Finder* (who stocks what) and *The Hillier Manual of Trees & Shrubs* (pithy descriptions) are the best, cheapest bibles followed by specialist catalogues like Thornhayes Nursery (the one we're looking at has 39 birches with the red-stemmed, orange and white), and that's before you get to Google. Then visit a specialist nursery, talk to the grower, get his advice and haggle.

Trees are sold according to their height, girth or container size, being available from one-year-old seedlings to monsters in 1000-litre containers. If you're used to perennials costing the same as a bottle of plonk, your fillings will ping out when you're quoted £4,000 for a 60-year-old cloud-pruned *Ilex crenata* (Japanese holly), all beautiful bare stubby stems and green tops. This is Xmas bonus instant gardening. Forget that. You'll need younger, cheaper plants for these projects. Plants that have to be trained.

Generally it's best to ask to see a **transplant** or a taller, feathered **maiden** or **whip**. Why?

First, they have a better chance of succeeding than the tall potted trees, say 5m (15ft) high. They'll soon catch them up, even though the "lamp posts" look like they're going to rocket away. What actually happens is that the latter sit around and boy, do they sulk, having been hauled out of their tight nursery rows or pots where they've been locked up for years. Second, these three are good sizes, being manageable and pliable; they require little staking and have a good balance of roots and shoots. Third, they're obviously cheaper than older trees. And fourth, the nurseryman will actually think you know what you're talking about. Only buy large for mega money when it's a slow-growing tree and you haven't got time to wait.

Transplant

Whip

Feathered maiden

Standard

THE TERMINOLOGY

Transplants Seedlings or cuttings which have been transplanted at least once, and are usually two to three years old.

Whips A young tree (seedling or grafted) with one single slender stem. Theoretically it's got no side branching, but might have some wispy side growth.

Maidens A young nursery tree that hasn't been pruned; can also refer to a woodland tree that hasn't been coppiced or pollarded.

Feathered trees With a central, upright, leading shoot and evenly spread lateral growth (the feathers) down the stem to near ground level, according to species.

Standards Trees with a single bare vertical stem pruned by nurserymen, and all the growth (the crown) at the top.

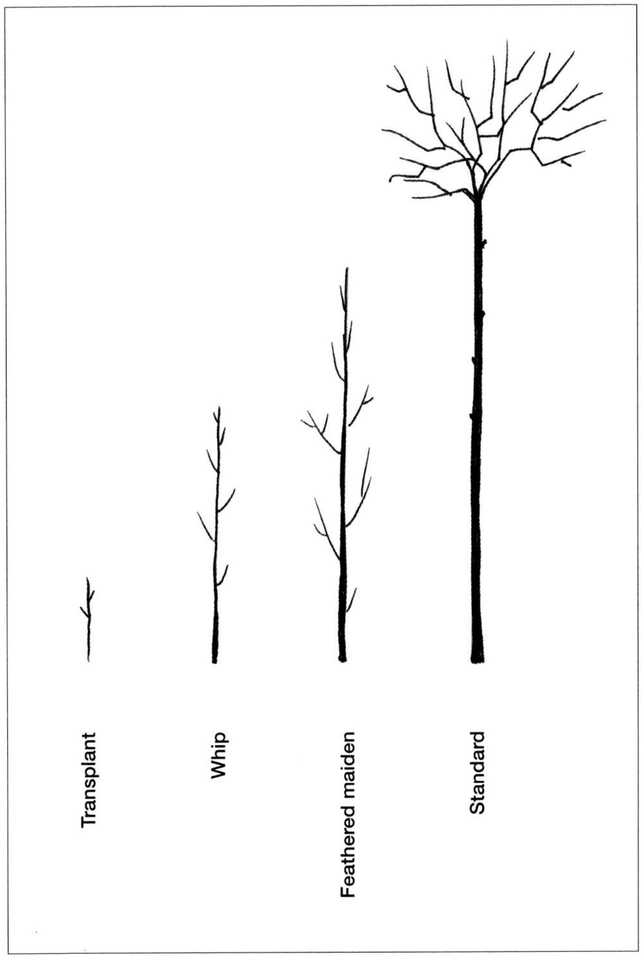

Note: It's immediately apparent to anyone researching the subject that books and catalogues don't give consistent figures for the above when it comes to height, which is why we're not using them. That'll ultimately depend on several factors, including which particular tree is being grown, and under what conditions, i.e. the location, soil conditions and number of times it has been transplanted, etc.

INTERPRETING CATALOGUES

This gives you a quick idea what to expect at a specialist nursery. Trees are available as three kinds: **bare root**, i.e. field-grown trees (rarely conifers) indicated as BR or FG (often bought mail order), sold when they've shed most of their leaves, obviously without any soil on the roots; **root-balled** or RB (also field-grown but lifted with a ball of soil around the roots); and **pot** or **container grown**.

BARE ROOT

The most economical way to buy trees is to locate a nursery specializing in hedging and forest trees. It'll list an extensive range of bare-root native and exotic species from 30cm (12in) high transplants. They are priced according to how many you need, e.g. from 1-9, 9-99, 100+ and 500+. Some nurseries want a minimum order of 10 of each sort.

Nurseries usually list the bare-root kind as "1 + 1" which means a 2-year old, transplanted after one year; "1 u 1" it means it has had two years in the ground, being undercut after one year. The act of transplanting prunes, or knocks off, the ends of the roots, encouraging more to grow, giving a well-branched spread. If the trees are left in the ground, undercutting does the same job. A machine runs along the rows of trees, and its underground "slicer" cuts off the ends of the roots below the surface. Larger, open-ground trees will have been undercut and transplanted during their nursery life.

Nurseries list their larger field-grown trees in girth sizes, again measured in centimetres at 1m (3½ft) above ground. So when you see...

6/8, 8/10, 10/12, 12/14, 16/18, etc.,

it means 6-8cm (2¼-3¼in). And these figures are doubly useful because the girth of a tree in centimetres roughly equates to the height of the tree in feet, so "6/8" means it's about 1.8-2.4m (6-8ft) high. (A similar trick for native parkland trees gives you their age. The girth in inches at breast height – 1.5m/5ft above ground – roughly equals the tree's age in years; trees in a wood put on 13mm/½in a year.) The larger trees are generally lifted with a rootball of soil and will be tagged "12/14 RB", "16/18RB", etc. Still with us?

When you buy, the main roots should ideally be outward-pointing and evenly spread (not all to one side and not in a tight coil), with an additional fuzzy mass of fibrous roots. But note, because willows and poplars will have been propagated from cuttings, the young plants may have roots from one side only because willow and poplar cuttings tend to initiate the first roots from one side.

Pros

- Available in a wide range of sizes.
- Available in quantity.
- The cheapest option.
- Will have been root-pruned to encourage fibrous roots.

Cons

- They're only available during the dormant season.
- Prone to drying out between lifting and delivery.

ROOT-BALLED TREES

Pros

- They generally transplant better than the bare-root kind.
- More expensive than the field-grown, but cheaper than the containerized kind.

Cons

- They need their balls kept moist. Avoid trees that have been left to dry out.
- Check that the root balls aren't loose and haven't been "made-up" because bare-root yews are sometimes "balled" by packing soil around them as a pudding. If you see an evergreen looking off colour, that's often the reason why. Even worse, because the foliage loses water by transpiration it may be dying when purchased, even though the soil is actually wet.

CONTAINER-GROWN TREES

They're available in all sizes and are listed by container size in litres, i.e. "C 25L", or "25L". Sometimes the girth and overall height/spread is included. Multi-stemmed trees are indicated as "MS".

When buying a container-grown tree, don't think you're exclusively buying the top growth. That's like buying a car without poking the engine. You're mainly paying for a good root system – and want to see plenty of spreading, healthy roots interspersed with wet soil – which is why all the books say "Slide it out the pot and check", though if you get a thick lip from the nurseryman don't blame us.

Pros

- They're usually available all year.
- Garden centres and nurseries now stock an extensive range of rare and unusual species.
- They're the best bet for some species which don't like being transplanted and hate root disturbance, e.g. most evergreens (holly and yew), and many exotic species.
- And they come with a guarantee that the tree is alive. If it is dead, take it back on a crowded Saturday morning and get shouting "IT'S DEAD". You'll get your money back but they'll probably kick you out.

Cons

- They're more expensive than the other kinds, and have restricted roots.
- Avoid anything with packed, thwarted roots bursting to escape the pot, when you can hardly see the soil.
- Ignore pots with self-strangling roots wrapped round and round the stem or, conversely, with a miserable, pathetic show of roots, or with

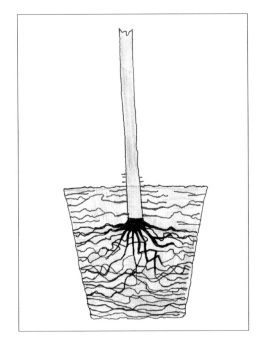

Deep planting produces an outbreak or roots (in red) where they're not wanted, above the normal root system. The sooner they're cut off and the tree is planted at the correct depth, the better. The root flare (the point where the required roots flare out) should be flush with, or fractionally above, ground level.

adventitious roots growing above soil level which means that the tree has been potted too deeply.

- Forget pots with neglected, dried out soil.
- Reject trees with feeble or damaged top growth, or lacking a good, even spread of branches.
- Check for vine weevils. The best way to detect if they're charging around like enemy submarines is to lift the tree gently by the stem. If the roots are being eaten, the tree will come away from the compost.
- Beware newly potted trees, i.e. field-grown trees that have recently been "containerized", and weren't container-grown, because their roots might not have grown into the compost. You're paying for a bare-root tree and a pot of compost, and the newly emerging roots might get damaged when replanting. The best way to check it's not newly potted is by gently lifting it out of the pot to see if the roots come clear of the soil.
- If in doubt, walk out.
- And loudly point out pots with an Amazonian display of weeds.

PLANTING

Container-grown trees can be bought and planted at any time, provided the weather is decent (i.e. forget extremes with droughts and frozen ground, etc.), but ideally in autumn. Water or stand the containers in a tub of cold water for 30 minutes before planting. The roots then need to be flicked and rummaged out with your fingers to encourage them to spread out, and to stop them from tunneling down in a spiral.

Bare-root and **root-balled** trees can be planted throughout the dormant season. When planting a root-balled tree, keep the ball intact and carefully get rid of what used to be called its hessian "sock"; it now tends to be made of nylon, even chicken wire, and could restrict the root growth, but again note that autumn is the best time. That's because the ground is still warm, and the roots will develop before the hard frosts and carry on growing next spring without a check. The root hairs are the drinking straws and the main roots are the anchors, so treat them with care. And because trees have been cut from the ground severing the ends of their roots, the remaining ones are prone to drying out and dying. Again, give them a long, pre-planting drink.

If you can't plant them for a few days or weeks, then dig a well-watered storage trench and get them in quick. Or securely prop them up and put their roots in a plastic bag and fill with moist compost and/or leafmould.

All kinds: The planting hole needs to be about three to four times the width of the roots or the pot, and 30cm (1ft) deep. Don't dig any deeper because (a) it's completely gratuitous, ninety per cent of tree roots stay close to the surface, and (b) you might as well barbecue the tree (or shrub) with a flame-thrower. Plant any deeper and it might take years and years to die while you wonder what the hell has gone wrong. In the past gardeners were encouraged to dig large luxury pits and fill them with compost and fertilizer. Don't do it. Be mean. These pits are potential death traps. They collect water, there'll be no oxygen, and the roots will rot. And when the organic matter starts rotting, the tree sinks lower in the ground. As for that "nose bag" of food, the pampered roots get lazy, don't extend to get a meal, and you can say goodbye to good anchorage. Pits shmits.

Now you've dug that hole, stab a fork in the bottom and give it a hefty wiggle to break up the soil and aid good drainage, but don't overdo it. Then stand the bare-root tree in place, making sure that the root flare or root collar (i.e. the point where the roots flare out) is flush with or just above ground level, and that the roots are nicely spread out in the hole so that the tree is well anchored. If you buy a container-grown tree, check it wasn't idiotically planted too deeply in its pot, with the root flare well down in the soil; if so, now's the time to save it by planting at the correct depth (see page 130).

Next, take a length of perforated pipe and loosely encircle the roots, so that the top will be sticking out of the soil at an angle. If necessary, fix the stake in position (see over). Then add fungi and fill the hole, adding mycorrhizal fungi (see page 155) to boost growth, and add a bucket of leafmould whether the soil is sand or clay. Then thump down the refill in layers so that the roots are wrapped round by soil and not by pockets of air. That's vital. Then heavily water in.

Finally, pile a 7.5cm (3in) well-rotted organic mulch around the trunk to lock in moisture and suppress weeds, but keep it away from the bark. Water well in dry weather until the tree is well-established by pouring water into the pipe end sticking out the ground, and it'll go straight to the roots. And keep grass, weeds and strimmers well away, at least 90cm (3ft) away from the trunk.

A mulch mat made from biodegradable jute, like an organic mulch, also blocks out grass. Even sheets of cardboard pegged down will do a decent job; when they rot and disintegrate, replace. Trees grow twice as fast without any competition for water and food.

If the planting position is on waterlogged ground, copy the Victorians. Fork over the ground and then build up the surface, making a 15cm (6in) high mound by adding topsoil, and plant here. Mounding should improve the drainage but, obviously, if the ground is really bad, what are you playing at?

Plant elsewhere. Also, when planting young evergreens in a cold, windy site, note that they may need protection for a couple of years.

Now some will yell, "Get real." And if you've 200 bare-root native trees to plant in a day, you're right. This does smack of la-di-da-TV-gardening that'd make professional gardeners spit. You can get away with spearing a spade in the ground, prizing it back to make a V-shape, and pushing the tree in the ground. But you can certainly do it better.

STAKING

Don't fret and stake young trees the moment the wind rattles them because a good wind-shake promotes strong stems and extra, anchoring root growth (grow a tree in a glass bubble and it'll be surprisingly weedy). Only stake when you're growing trees over 1.8-2.4m (6-8ft) high, and then for a maximum of 14 months. If there's a persistent wind slamming across open country, don't stake and grow small trees instead.

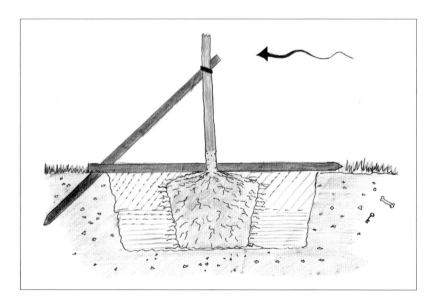

Use a horizontal pole to check that the top of the roots are virtually at ground level, and angle the stake into the prevailing wind. Use trees ties, and never string. Make sure they never cut into the bark, and don't forget to remove them when the tree is stable.

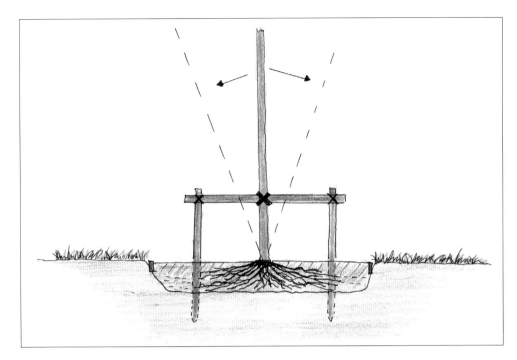

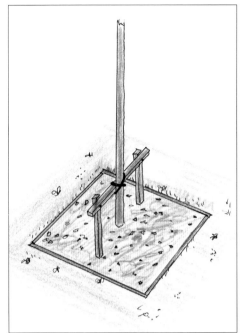

If you don't think the single stake method is working, and that the tree is working loose, try a cross-beam. It still allows for some movement but gives more stability.

Use a sturdy length of wood, about one-third of the tree's height, with 30cm (1ft) showing above ground, whacked into the ground before planting at 45 degrees to the trunk, which will keep the roots locked and steady. Don't forget and do it later in case you spear the roots. And make sure the stake's top points into the prevailing wind so that the top growth sways away from the stake, and doesn't splinter against it.

PRUNING AND TRAINING

Deciduous trees are best shaped in midwinter, when you have a clear sight of what needs doing. Wait three months, until mid-spring, before tackling evergreens.

Be kind to your tree. Make it happy.

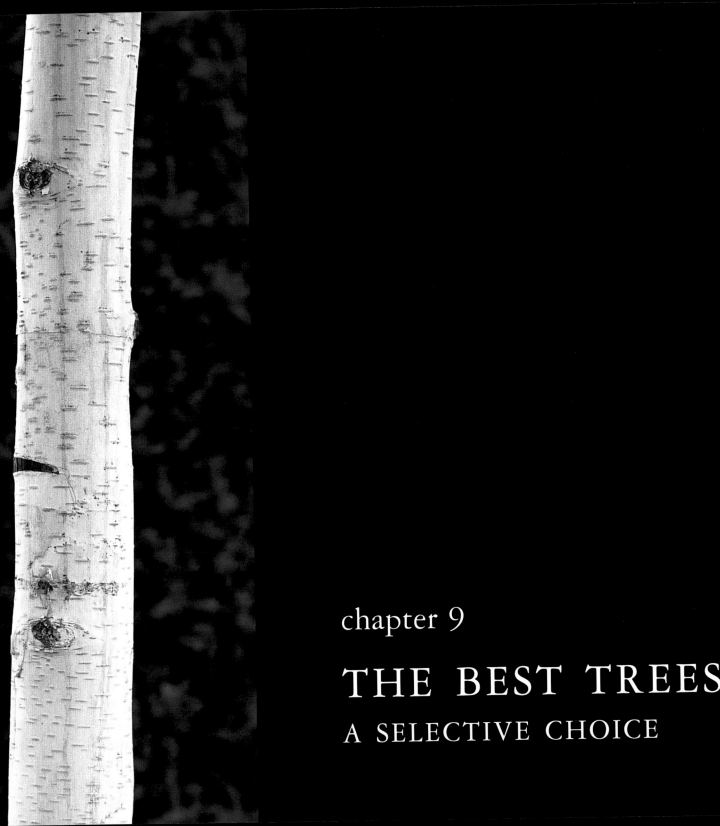

chapter 9

THE BEST TREES

A SELECTIVE CHOICE

The following can be used as singles, pairs, avenues and circles, etc., and many of the more pliable species can be used for training or manipulation, or coppicing or pollarding. The heights refer to average, eventual, unhindered growth in ideal conditions, often after many decades.

ACER (MAPLE)

Ranging from small- to medium-size Japanese maples (*A. palmatum* and *A. japonicum*) with highly distinctive, often delicate foliage and flashy autumn colours to the larger maples and sycamores. The latter are desperately dull, but they are tough city and coastal survivors with a dense crown. Cut them back and they resprout strongly.

Most maples are easily grown in most soils, even clay. The Japanese kind prefer deep soil - not thin, chalky ground — and shelter from cold winds is vital or the young foliage scorches. Autumn colour is often best on acid soil. All acers have opposite buds and are flexible, making them ideal for training into shapes.

A. platanoides (Norway maple) — fast-growing tree when young, putting on 2m (6½ft) a year with autumn leaves flaring bright yellow; in hot, dry years, on acid soil, often orange. Note the bright yellow-green flowers on bare branches in early spring. 25m (80ft). The excellent 'Globosum' at 6m (20ft) high is good in limited spaces; the purple-leaved forms (e.g. 'Crimson King') are ridiculously over-planted and form great blotches of gloomy, funereal foliage when mature.

A. pseudoplatanus (sycamore) — gutsy, determined tree that'll grow just about anywhere, even by the sea; immune to gales and salt. Good for coppicing and pollarding, and for clumps and screens. The winged seeds can sprout even inside old, hollow trees. 35m (115ft)

A. p. 'Brilliantissimum' — the slower growing, more compact form if you like new leaves turning from bright pink to yellow-green to green. Most love it ... 6m (20ft)

A. rubrum (Canadian or red maple) — scarlet leaves in autumn, especially on acid soil. Avoid chalk or the colour will be yellow. 18m (60ft)

A. r. 'October Glory' — as its name suggests. 15m (50ft)

A. r. 'Scanlon' — compact, branching habit. 15m (50ft)

A. saccharinum (silver maple) — graceful, thinly branched, with deeply lobed leaves, light green on top and silvery underneath. Best when the long, thin shoots and branches get wind-whipped, the two colours flapping about. Good early autumn tints. 23m (75ft)

A. saccharum (sugar maple) — initially quick growing; has smart autumn colours – crimson, red, orange or yellow – but if you're expecting a New England show outside the USA, no way, Europe can't compete. New kinds now available from specialist nurseries which may improve the show. 21m (70ft)

SNAKEBARK MAPLES

Essential. The striking, striated bark can be washed with a soft brush to remove algae, highlighting the effect. Being medium size they are ideal for small gardens, and have fantastic autumn colour.

A. capillipes – red young growth, shiny leaves and silver stripes. Arching branches. 10m (30ft)

A. davidii (Père David's maple) – silver stripes. 15m (50ft)

A. d. 'George Forest' – more vigorous form with flashy red leaf stalks. 15m (50ft)

A. grosseri – white stripes turning greyish. 8m (25ft) but...

A. g. var. *hersii* is the most widely available form. 7m (22ft)

A. henryi – bluish stripes. 8m (25ft)

A. pensylvanicum – white and green stripes turning reddish-brown. 11m (35ft)

AILANTHUS ALTISSIMA (TREE OF HEAVEN)

You'd be raving not to grow one. Fast-growing tree with leaves (composed of leaflets) up to 60cm (2ft) long, but cut back hard to just above soil level each autumn and next spring you'll have leaves twice as big; keep to a single stem. Use with other large-leaved plants (figs, *Paulownia tomentosa* and *Tetrapanax papyrifer*). Tolerates pollution and most soils, but shelter from battering winds. The male flowers reek. 21m (70ft)

ALNUS (ALDER)

Tough, easily grown trees doing well in most soils, especially damp ground, and by water.

A. cordata (Italian alder) – tall, narrow-crowned tree, fast-growing when young at 1m (3½ft) a year, with a long season of bright green, glossy leaves. Has late winter 10-15cm (4-6in) long purple catkins. Super tough and grows anywhere; on top of a chalky hill or at the water's edge. Good in avenues. 23m (75ft)

BETULA (BIRCH)

Real toughies – pioneer trees – found in extreme situations. Top choice for a fast-growing, graceful tree with striking bark. As in the wild, they look best *en masse*; forget loners. Plant in pairs, groups, or short, narrow avenues. Buy a multi-stemmed specimen or plant three or more young trees in the same hole to create the same effect. In the wild, this multi-stemmed effect is often caused by animals nibbling young trees, making them branch low down; hard pruning or coppicing a young tree gets the same result. Otherwise, don't prune or top because it'll look hideous.

Birches grow in the poorest soils and officially hate thin, chalky ground but you often find them growing there, though their size might suffer. Except for the river birch (*B. nigra*) and *B. pubescens*, keep away from water. Note: Don't get fobbed off with downy birch (*B. pubescens*) that's easily confused with silver birch (*B. pendula*) when young. The key difference is that downy birch has fine hairs on the twig ends, silver birch being rough to finger and thumb.

B. albosinensis (Chinese birch) – peeling bark ranging from copper red to pink. 25m (80ft)

B. nigra (river birch) – fast-growing and one of the best

birches for wet ground, but also happy in loamy soil. The shaggy bark changes from pinkish-buff to dark brown, peeling off in long tatters. Keep six-year-olds away or there'll be nothing left. The deep yellowish autumn leaves hang on, giving a good show. 18m (60ft)

B. n. 'Heritage' – a new form selected for its peeling, creamy bark. 18m (60ft)

B. utilis (Himalayan birch) – variable in the wild; the thin, peeling bark ranges from mahogany to white. 18m (60ft)

B. u. 'Fascination' – new form with deep orange peeling bark revealing layers of variable colours.

B. u. var. *jacquemontii* – the Big One for a flash of white, standing out in winter with stiff, upward-angled branches. Fine-tune by periodically peeling off the bark for new layers of egg white. If the trunk gets mud splattered or covered in algae, wash off with warm water and a soft brush. 18m (60ft)

B. u. var. *j.* 'Grayswood Ghost', 'Jermyns' – the best forms of the species but not always easily available, and therefore expensive. 18m (60ft)

CARPINUS BETULUS (HORNBEAM)

Tough trees, good for pollarding and everything from hedging to topiary, arches, arbours and pleaching, etc. Highly rated for their attractive shape and autumn colours. Equally good on thin, chalky soils or heavy clay. Often confused with beech.

C. betulus 'Fastigiata' – more wide-bottomed and pyramidal than pointed; each main branch springs from the trunk to form a shaving brush effect. 14m (46ft)

C. b. 'Frans Fontaine' – fastigiate, growing like a tight

Lombardy poplar (*Populus nigra* 'Italica'). Excellent for narrow avenues or green structures (e.g. arches). 14m (46ft)

CATALPA BIGNONIOIDES (INDIAN BEAN TREE)

The long seedpods shake and rattle in the wind; are dried and painted by native Americans for decoration (forget India, it comes from the Deep South). Makes a low, wide-spreading tree with large, heart-shaped leaves (appearing late) and white flowers (late summer). Can be hard pruned or coppiced for bigger leaves, but you won't get any flowers. Only for milder parts of the country and inner cities. Good for dry soils and hot summers. 15m (50ft)

C. b. 'Aurea' – slightly shorter, with translucent, pale yellow leaves, but you'll never spot the white flowers. 8m (25ft)

CERCIDIPHYLLUM JAPONICUM

The autumn leaves give great lungfuls of toffee apples and burnt sugar. Delightful small tree from southern Japan and China with rounded, soft green leaves turning yellowish and pink in autumn. Impressively multi-stemmed, but can easily be pruned to a single trunk. Happy in moist ground; hates drought. 19m (60ft)

C. j. 'Rotfuchs' – deep purple, sumptuous foliage. 5m (16ft)

COTONEASTER FRIGIDUS 'CORNUBIA'

Typically a large shrub but also sold as a small tree; can be trained as a single or multi-stem specimen. Easily forms a huge green mushroom – barnacled bright red because of the massive amount of large fruit – which you can sit on top of, especially if you plant four close together. Otherwise excellent for rapid, evergreen growth (semi-evergreen in cold, exposed gardens), giving good cover or screening. Smothered by small, white summer flowers. The bunches of red fruit weigh down the branches, and hang on through winter. Likes well-drained soil. 6m (20ft)

CRATAEGUS (HAWTHORN)

A small can-survive-anything thorny tree that'll take a hammering from inner cities, coasts and winters in the wild, and anywhere in between including wet, dry or poor, chalky ground. Late spring white flowers and masses of red berries for the birds. Can be topiarized, clipped, and trained any-whichway.

C. crus-galli var. *pyracanthifolia* – forms a perfect low umbrella shape without the need for pruning. 3.5m (11½ft)

C. persimilis "Prunifolia' – compact, dome-shaped crown, twiggy and tangled, with oval leaves, white flowers and bright red fruit. Electric autumn leaves, all reds and orange; they start "ripening" on one side of the tree, moving across, giving a long show of colour. Also grown as a moundy bush. 6m (20ft)

C. phaenepoyrum – the highly distinctive, round-headed Washington thorn has shiny, maple-like leaves, white flowers in the first part of summer, and shiny, dark red fruit. Good orange-red autumn colour. 10m (30ft)

C. tanacetifolia – excellent thornless hawthorn with dissected, silvery leaves, apple-like orange-yellow fruit, and white, scented midsummer flowers. 5m (16ft)

DAVIDIA INVOLUCRATA (HANKERCHIEF TREE)

Gets its name from the large white bracts in the branches. Takes a few years to flower, but spectacular. No autumn colour. Hates drought. 14m (46ft)

EUCALYPTUS (GUM)

Buy one. All have grey-green evergreen foliage, many with sensational, beautiful bark. Plant when small, and never buy a large one or you'll have to stake it forever because they quickly get top heavy, but you can prune hard to generate new growth lower down, or pollard. Excellent for seaside or dry soil, but don't even think about chalk.

E. pauciflora subsp. *niphophila* (snow gum) – fantastic short tree with a python's skin of patchwork, flaking bark in mottled green, cream and grey. 6m (20ft)

FAGUS SYLVATICA (COMMON BEECH)

Huge forest trees making the perfect, deciduous hedge with gorgeous autumn foliage which hangs on ginger, crisp and withered; can be clipped into hedges, shapes, arches, etc. The copper-leaved forms are variable because they are grown from seed, so go for a grafted, named variety, especially 'Riversii' with large leaves and rich colour. The young leaves are wine red; occasional summer trimming promotes a regular supply. Likes chalk or free-draining soil in sun or shade.

F. s. 'Dawyck', 'Dawyck Purple' – thin, columnar shapes (the former is green leaved, the latter purple), popular with trendy designers. 20m (65ft)

F. s. var. *heterophylla* – distinctive, medium-size tree with dissected, fern-like leaves. Slower growing than common beech. 15m (50ft)

F. s. 'Pendula' (weeping beech) – spectacular large tree with horizontal and hanging branches, creating curtain-like effect. 23m (75ft)

F. s. 'Zlatia' (golden beech) – excellent form with soft yellow new foliage turning green in summer. Avoid exposed situations. 20m (65ft)

FICUS CARICA (FIG)

Monster 25cm (10in) long leaves and tasty fruit (from the spring crop, not the one starting in midsummer which doesn't have enough time to ripen outside) if given a hot spot against a wall. For extra fruit, remove the branch tips in mid-spring but leave on the young figs; this generates new sideshoots which need cutting back to four leaves in early summer. Can be trained into fantastic shapes because of the pliable, rubbery growth. Needs a restricted root-run, either in a large tub from 38-60cm (15–24in) wide and deep, or in a pit with broken bricks at the bottom though the roots nearly always escape. Alternatively, grow freestanding and forget the fruit. Good varieties include 'Brunswick' and 'Desert King'. 5m (16ft)

FRAXINUS (ASH)

Large and fast-growing; most soils and situations, including coasts and polluted cities, are fine.

F. angustifolia 'Raywood' – dense, compact, upright tree with dark green foliage turning plummy purple in autumn. Superb, narrow-leaved ash. 21m (70ft)

KOELREUTERIA PANICULATA (GOLDEN RAIN TREE)

The golden rain refers to the upright panicles of yellow flowers, about 25cm (10in) long, in late summer. The long, attractive leaves are flushed pink in spring and turn yellow-orange in autumn. Needs a hot, dry place. 10m (30ft)

LABURNUM X *WATERERI* '*VOSSII*' (GOLDEN RAIN)

A tough, small tree with pliable growth. Can easily be manipulated, and that's why it's often used for tunnels and arches where its long, bunched flowers hang down in great gobbets of yellow. Plant five young trees in a semi-circle 2–3m diameter (6½–10ft) to make a golden arbour. Likes most soils. 8m (25ft)

LIQUIDAMBER STYRACIFLUA (SWEET GUM)

Gardening cocaine. Large tree with brash autumn colour, but 'Worplesdon' (orange) and 'Lane Roberts' (blackish-crimson) are even better. Sensational in most soils. 23m (75ft)

LIRIODENDRON TULIPIFERA (TULIP TREE)

Bizarrely shaped leaves turning yellow and russet in autumn.

Tulip-like, yellowish-green-orange flowers on older trees. Likes slightly acid, moist ground; avoid thin, chalk soil. 30m (100ft).

L. t. 'Fastigiatum' – forms a narrow, cypress-like tree. 21m (70ft)

MAGNOLIA GRANDIFLORA

Giant, eye-grabbing glossy leaves and, if you wait a few years, boxing-glove-size, waxy flowers from midsummer to autumn – not prolific, but who cares – smelling of lemon and melon. Generally grown against a sheltering, sunny wall, but possible in the open in sheltered sites. Grows like a weed in Italy. To 17m (55ft).

M. g. 'Exmouth' – free-flowering from an early age.
M. g. 'Goliath' – even larger flowers.

MALUS (CRAB APPLE)

Vast range of ornamental crab and eating/dessert apples. The cooking kind are easily trained and manipulated into all kinds of fantastic shapes to maximize the amount of fruit, and the ornamental ones can be similarly treated. As a general rule, winter pruning of longer shoots to 3 to 4 buds creates spurs with flowering/fruiting buds. Just a few apple trees carry fruit on their tips; prune the older, tired long shoots that have been fruiting for years, cutting back to new, young sideshoots. The pruning cycle keeps replacing the old fruiting growth with the new. Hates soggy ground. Avoid the yellow-fruiting *M.* x *zumi* 'Golden Hornet' which turns mushy brown in the first frost.

M. x *robusta* 'Red Sentinel' – excellent small tree with pinkish flowers followed by cherry-red crab-apples persisting through winter. Two make a stunning arch. 6m (20ft)

MORUS NIGRA (BLACK MULBERRY)

Takes 20 years to get a crop of fruit; juicy, delicious, but you'll have to fight off the birds. Also good foliage tree. Average, we'll-drained soil. Make sure you get *M. nigra*, not *M. alba*. The former gives delicious fruit, *M. alba* a washed-out, indsipid crop. 11m (35ft)

PAULOWNIA TOMENTOSA (FOXGLOVE TREE)

Mega leaves, 30cm (12in) long, and erect, foxglove-like flowers smelling of violets in hot, sunny sites. To get larger, more pumped-up leaves, coppice hard back in spring forcing out vigorous shoots growing 2m (6½ft) high or more, with leaves like giant poppadums, 90cm (3ft) wide. Best on sunny sites with rich soil; feed and water well, then again, and again, and don't let up all summer, but also seen growing on bone dry soil and in walls in the South of France. If exposed to ripping winds the leaves get shredded. 12m (40ft)

PLATANUS (PLANE TREE)

Magnificent, huge trees, frequently planted in cities in the nineteenth century because they tolerate pollution. Its three best-known forms are...

P. x *hispanicus* (London plane) – too vast and monumental for most gardens, each one needing 0.2ha (0.6 acres), which they didn't realize when planting up city streets, and a real powerhouse of a survivor. Grows fast in any situation, is long-lived, and never gets blown down, but can be used to create extraordinary forms because it responds well to pollarding. The flaking bark creates marbled patterning, and each tree is different. Those in London's Berkeley Square were planted in 1789. 30m (100ft)

P. occidentalis (American sycamore, buttonwood) – don't waste your time in the UK. Doesn't succeed.

P. orientalis (Oriental plane) – extremely responsive to pollarding.

POPULUS

A huge genus of fast-growing trees, good for wet sites and most soils but generally avoid thin chalky soil.

P. alba (white poplar) – felty grey leaves, white underneath, and stunning when they flap in the wind. Yellow-autumn colour. Grows well almost anywhere, even near the sea and on chalky soils. Prolific suckering. Being flexible can be used to make simple shapes, or coppice and grow as a dramatic, large shrub. 36m (120ft)

P. lasiocarpa (Chinese necklace tree) – a gem of a tree, it gets its name from the 30cm (12in) long catkins festooning the tree in midsummer. Spectacular bright green leaves, also 30cm (12in) long with red veining and leaf stalks. Hard prune to generate even larger leaves. Often grown grafted on a leg, so beware suckers and promptly remove them. 21m (70ft)

P. tremula (quaking aspen) – leaves on long stalks which quiver in the slightest breeze, colouring clear yellow in autumn. Suckers appear from the roots, forming a thicket of trees if left. Very pliable and easily trained or "welded" together. 18m (60ft)

PRUNUS (ORNAMENTAL CHERRY)

Large genus including almonds, apricots, cherries, peaches and plums. Also scores of ornamental Japanese cherries producing a great frothy blast of spring blossom, pink or white. Few rivals, and all have good autumn colour. Avoid pruning because they respond badly and look ugly.

P. avium (gean, wild cherry) – the native woodland wild cherry is a strong-growing tree with polished, reddish-brown, peeling bark and single, white, mid-spring flowers and cherries quickly taken by birds (hence *avium*). Easily overlooked in favour of the candyfloss kind, but a magnificent tall tree with one main stem, good for avenues, and fantastic autumn colour. 22m (72ft)

P. padus (bird cherry) – an unfamiliar, tough native. Late spring flowers in white spikes, almond scented. 11m (35ft)

P. padus 'Colorata' – a fantastic form with blackish-copper-purple foliage in spring (turning dark green) and pink flowers. 11m (35ft)

P. serrula (Tibetan cherry) – *The* tree with spit'n'polish-shiny-brown bark, not apparent until the growth is broomstick thick. Enhanced by gentle peeling. Critics say "Sparse flowering for a cherry." Who cares? Excellent in small space. 6m (20ft)

P. 'Shirotae' – also called 'Mount Fuji', a superb tree with scented, pure white flowers and apple green foliage. Wider than high, with horizontal branches; puffs up to a white cloud in full flower. Orange, yellow and red autumn colours. 6m (20ft)

PTEROCARYA X REHDERANA (WING NUT)

Large, fast-growing – and we mean fast – suckering tree for most soils, and good by water. Large leaves and attractive, persistent catkins. 23m (75ft)

QUERCUS (OAK)

Where to start? Over 100 species and forms, and that's just in the UK. Need deep, rich ground so forget thin chalky soil. Excellent near the sea. Alphabetically, the top five are:

Q. *coccinea* (scarlet oak) – large tree with pointy, lobed leaves turning scarlet in autumn. 21m (70ft)

Q. *frainetto* (Hungarian oak) – huge tree, fast growing with large leaves. Good on all soils including chalk. 29m (95ft)

Q. *ilex* (holm oak) – ubiquitous in churches and parks, at its best in early summer with new, silvery, sage green leaves. Excellent near the sea. Good for pyramids and mopheads. 23m (75ft)

Q. *robur* (common or English oak) – who needs anything else? Tough, spreading, with twisting branches. Good on clay. Said to host 350 insects against a sycamore's 16. 36.5m (120ft)

Q. *r.* 'Fastigiata Koster' – narrow column for focal points. 15m (50ft)

ROBINIA PSEUDOACACIA (BLACK LOCUST)

Wonderful, billowing clumping heads of foliage and white pea-like summer flowers on mature trees. Because of the brittle branches, (a) it needs a sheltered position and (b) isn't good for training, but lopped branches give great clouds of new foliage. 25m (80ft)

R. *p.* 'Bessononia' - a natural, rounded mophead. Fun for smaller gardens. 15m (50ft), as is …

R. *p.* 'Frisia' - the yellow-leaf form is over planted, but gives good, clear colour all summer and turns orange-yellow in autumn. 15m (50ft)

SALIX (WILLOW)

A huge range from whopping trees to tiny shrubs, generally quick growing. Very flexible; they respond well to hard or regular pruning. Most willows grow in damp conditions and in all soils, except thin chalk.

S. *alba* (white willow) – large, graceful tree with slender branches and billowing masses of silvery green leaves. A waterside "must". 23m (75ft)

S. *babylonica* var. *pekinensis* 'Tortuosa' (contorted willow) – writhing tracery of twisty-twirly stems. Flower arrangers' fodder. 15m (50ft)

S. x *sepulcralis* var. *chrysocoma* (weeping willow) – curtains of hanging branches and shoots, sulphur yellow in spring when the catkins appear just before the leaves, and one of the first trees to flush. Foliage often hangs on in winter. Can be pruned hard by shortening the main branches by half. 15m (50ft)

The best for coloured new stems which flash out in winter, and to be coppiced every two years to maintain a fresh supply – though you can remove half the stems one year, the rest the next year – include ...

S. alba 'Cardinalis' – deep red.

S. a. var. *vitellina* 'Britzensis' – the pick of the bunch. Striking orange-scarlet; also makes a very good tree. 15m (50ft). Often listed by lazy nurseryman as 'Chermesina'; var. *vitellina* is bright yellow.

S. daphnoides – plum-red with white bloom. 'Aglaia' is red but no bloom.

S. purpurea 'Nancy Saunders' – shiny red with narrow, blue-green leaves.

S. viminalis – rapid, long, olive/yellow green new growth.

SORBUS ARIA (WHITEBEAM)

A tough, attractive tree (seen in city parks and streets) that'll grow anywhere on free-draining soil. Upright branches, then spreading. Excellent for windy or coastal gardens. Thrives on chalky and acid soil. For larger leaves try 'Lutescens' and *S. thibetica* 'John Mitchell'. 5m (16ft). Also try ...

S. hupehensis – small tree from Western China with blue-green leaves turning shades of crimson in autumn, falling before the white, persistent fruit (ignored by birds). Prefers deeper soil. 5m (16ft)

TILIA (LIME)

Tough, city-hardy trees growing in most soils and situations: can be coppiced, pollarded or pleached. Have sweet-scented, bee-attracting, white to yellow summer flowers.

T. cordata 'Swedish Upright' – the narrow form of the British native, small-leaved lime. Good for avenues. Hunt down from specialist nurseries. 18m (60ft)

T. henryana – stunning, slow-growing Chinese tree with buff-pink new leaves turning green, and whitish autumn flowers. 13m (42ft)

CONIFERS

ABIES (FIR)

The firs are mostly medium to large forest trees. Some wrongly call all conifers fir trees, but the true firs are easily identified when mature. Their cones are erect and break apart to release seed while still on the tree, whereas the cones of spruces (*Picea*) are egg-shaped and hang down before falling intact.

A. koreana (Korean fir) – small, slow-growing, narrow pyramid with dark green foliage and silvery white needles beneath. Produces clustered violet cones or barrels even when quite young, before 10 years old. 10m (30ft)

ARAUCARIA ARAUCANA (MONKEY PUZZLE)

Popular in the nineteenth century when seed arrived in the UK from South America. It was used as a dot plant, then became the tree everybody hated but it's now "in" again for its spiky leaves and spare, prehistoric look and rigidly upright, single trunk that'll never fork. Becomes pyramidal. Excellent in avenues. Prefers good, deep soil. 18m (60ft)

CALOCEDRUS DECURRENS (INCENSE CEDAR)

Not a true cedar – it gets its name from the scented wood – and forms a fantastic bright green column, from 2m (6½ft) wide, looking like a green pencil. Plant in groups. 30m (100ft)

CEDRUS (CEDAR)

Huge, wide-spreading trees. Mature cedars have a number of boles and are virtually giant bushes.

C. atlantica (Atlas cedar) – ascending branches. Fast growing when young, and similar to the slower *C. libani*. The intense blue-grey Glauca Group is the best. Initially slow growing.35m (115ft)

C. deodara (Himalayan cedar) – drooping branches with bluish-grey young leaves. Quick sprinter and easily pruned. 35m (115ft)

C. libani (Lebanon Cedar) – level, tiered branches, eventually making a flat-topped specimen. Some on Mount Lebanon are 2,500 years old, with a 14.6m (48ft) circumference. Many prefer the bluer *C. a.* Glauca Group. Sprints up when young. Needs good drainage. 30m (100ft).

CHAMAECYPARIS LAWSONIANA
(LAWSON OR FALSE CYPRESS)

Closely related to the true cypress (*Cupressus*) but with flat, frond-like branches. Impossible to make a decent recommendation: hundreds of varieties (selling better than the species), with yellowish, blue or green leaves, some virtually indistinguishable. Provide good drainage and moist soil. If research drives you crackers, try:

C. l. 'Columnaris Glauca' - slim, grey-blue column; every designers' "accent plant". Thinner on poor, dry ground, wider on richer soil. Fast growing. 12m (40ft)

C. l. 'Green Hedger' – accurately named; good for hedging and screening with upright, dense, emerald green foliage. 14m (46ft)

C. l. 'Pembury Blue' – silvery blue foliage, forming a conical shape. 14m (46ft)

C. nootkatensis – tough, slim Alaskan tree, and one of the parents of Leyland cypress (see over). Dark green foliage droops down from the branches. 25m (82ft)

C. l. n. 'Glauca' – as above but with distinctive, blue-green foliage. 25m (82ft)

CRYPTOMERIA (JAPANESE CEDAR)

Not a true cedar but a large – and we mean huge – Japanese/Chinese tree resembling redwoods, with a single, powerful, red-barked, peeling trunk. Invariably bronze leaves in winter.

C. japonica Elegans Group – sold for its fuzzy, feathery juvenile foliage, green in summer turning rich purple-rust in winter. The colder it is, the better the colour. Good (or outrageously twee) contrast with yellow conifers; the sunnier the site the better the purple. Initially upright, then sprawls. Shelter from cold, blasting winds. 18m (60ft)

X CUPRESSOCYPARIS LEYLANDII (LEYLAND CYPRESS)

Stunning tree, inheriting hardiness and vigour from its parents. It'll fly up at 1m (3½ft) a year for say 20 years, then at 60cm (2ft) a year, making two-thirds of Nelson's column or more, and that's why it's a nightmare when a bolshy neighbour grows one as an unpruned boundary hedge in countries without a legal maximum hedge height. You can stop it at hedge height, trimming twice a year, slowing it down, keeping it at say 1.8m (6ft). 30m (100ft)

GINKGO BILOBA (MAIDENHAIR TREE)

The only surviving species from the *Ginkgoales* which were ubiquitious 150–200 million years ago. Now popular in cities, and good in avenues. Invariably upright with thick, fan-like leaves turning bright gold in autumn. If you get a female it'll have blue-green fruit, turning orange-brown. The decomposing smell is vile but that's no excuse for saying "Not gonna grow one." The male 'Autumn Gold' has good autumn colour. 40m (130ft)

LARIX (LARCH)

Decidious, twiggy conifers forming tall, fast-growing trees. (All conifers are evergreen except for larch, metasequoia and taxodium.) Fresh green foliage in spring turning bright yellow to orange in autumn. Well-drained soil.

L. decidua (European larch) – graceful, horizontal branches and quick to leaf out in spring before most other trees. Turns butter yellow in autumn. Good in a circle, showering golden needles in autumn. Steer clear of *L. d.* 'Corley'; it's a midget for rock gardens. 30m (100ft)

METASEQUOIA GLYPTOSTROBOIDES (DAWN REDWOOD)

A powerhouse rocket of an ancient, deciduous tree, discovered in 1941 in south-west China, causing a sensation. Thought to have been extinct for millions of years. Has shaggy, ginger brown bark and yew-like foliage turning pinkish-russet in autumn. Leaves appear early and hang on until late autumn. Shelter and long hot summers without a drought give best results. Avoid chalk. Plant young specimens because bigger ones hate being transplanted. A few clones from Canada and Holland are now available. 30m (100ft)

PICEA (SPRUCE)

Large forest trees, often too big for gardens, preferring cool, moist condition. Avoid cities, coasts and chalk.

P. abies (Norway spruce, Christmas tree) – grown for timber and paper-making. Many new selections are now available, but most make slow-growing dwarfs for the rock garden. 39.6m (130ft)

If you want a Christmas tree there are much better choices, with the Nordmann fir (*Abies nordmanniana*), Fraser's fir (*A. fraseri*) and Scots pine (*Pinus sylvestris*) all good at briefly withstanding sitting-room conditions. The best way to keep a Christmas tree happy is to buy it pot grown (not recently containerized) with a root system so it can drink and the leaves won't dry and drop. Keep inside, well away from a radiator, for about 10 days maximum, then plant out. The chopped-off kind should be treated like cut flowers. Saw out a 5mm (¼in) wedge in the bottom to break the tree's self-protective seal, and wedge the trunk in pebbles in a bucket with water, and it'll suck up a pint a day. You can buy anti-dessicant sprays to minimize leaf-fall, but keep the Dyson ready.

P. omorika (Serbian spruce) – fast-growing, narrow, graceful tree with up-curving branches and rich green leaves. Grows well on all soils, including chalk. Tolerates pollution. 20m (70ft)

PINUS (PINE)

Huge genus with needle-like foliage. Many are good for poor, dry soils in windy or coastal sites (*P. nigra, P. pinaster* and *P. sylvestris*). The three- and five-needle pines generally prefer better soil.

P. coulteri (big cone pine) – really big cones, up to 30cm (1ft) long and weighing more than 2kg (4.4lb), and long needles. 25m (82ft)

P. parviflora 'Tempelhof' – eventually flat-topped, with blue-grey foliage. 6m (20ft)

P. patula (Mexican pine) – don't be put off by its Mexican origins, this is a tough beauty that'll hit 10m (30ft) in a decade. Can be stopped at 1.5m (5ft) high, and grown in a single row making a filtered screen with beautiful clusters of 20cm (8in) long, thin, soft needles. Keep pruning for shape. The cinnamon bark cracks open low-down to reveal reddish-brown. Cold winds frazzle the needles brown. 15m (50ft)

P. sylvestris Aurea Group – a small, slow-growing form of Scots pine (they're all tenacious, capable of growing on rocky ground) with bright yellow foliage, good in winter. Prune the tip to encourage a wide, low head. 6m (20ft)

P. wallichiana (Bhutan pine) – elegant pine with 20cm (8in) long needles and large 25cm (10in) banana-shaped cones. Most soils. 25m (82ft)

SCIADOPITYS VERTICILLATA
(JAPANESE UMBERELLA PINE)

A small, slow-growing southern Japanese tree with long, thick, rigid, shiny needles in whorls, like miniature umbrella spokes, at the ends of the shoots. Looks good in a large container, especially when old and the reddish bark peels. Instant bonsai. Acid soil, needs good wind shelter. Avoid dry ground. 20m (65ft)

SEQUOIA SEMPERVIRENS
(COASTAL/CALIFORNIAN REDWOOD)
SEQUOIADENDRON GIGANTEUM
(WELLINGTONIA/GIANT REDWOOD)

Both are called giant redwoods because of their width and gargantuan, powering height; they have similar rust red, finger-deep spongy bark that children keep trying to rip off.

The world's tallest tree is a coastal redwood – the

'Stratosphere Giant' – at 112.34m (368ft 7in) when measured in the 1990s. There is one example of a cut stump with 2,200 rings, and since shoots can grow from low down, regenerating from a cut stump, some trees roots may be even older than the top growth. 'General Sherman', a giant redwood, is the world's largest living thing at 82.6m (271ft) high and 5,440 tons, while 'Grizzly Giant' gets a longevity prize being about 3,400 years old. (The world's oldest tree is apparently a 4,600-year-old bristlecone pine in California.) In the UK some redwoods are now almost 50m (164ft) high since being planted in the mid-nineteenth century. Note: *S. sempervirens* prefers to be grown amongst other trees to prevent winter wind scorch, while *S. giganteum* will stand alone getting full exposure. Most situations except thin chalky soils.

TAXODIUM DISTICHUM (SWAMP CYPRESS)

Often confused with *Metasequoia*, it's excellent for wet sites – plant on a mound and, when mature, the cypress produces strange, hollow, breathing roots (pneumatophores) that project out of the water. Reddish-brown bark. Best in autumn when it turns rust red. Widespread in the Florida Everglades. 25m (80ft)

TAXUS BACCATA (YEW)

The mother of all (churchyard) UK trees, with the largest girth and ultimate age (commonly 1,000 years old but some are hanging on, being about 5,000 years old). The tallest tend to be young and woodland-sheltered. The wood is strong and elastic, and even when the bole has hollowed out trees keep standing and don't collapse. Excellent and indestructible for tall hedges and topiary, and makes a dark green background for brighter planting. A row of saplings can be arched over, and where the tips touch the ground, they'll root, making a tunnel. Not as slow growing as often suggested, taking a year or two to establish, then putting on 30cm (1ft) a year. Many forms available. Toxic. Good for all soils (including chalk and clay) but dislike getting their feet wet. 15m (50ft)

THUJA PLICATA (WESTERN RED CEDAR)

Not a true cedar but grown for aromatic greenhouse timber and cladding (and in North American for canoes and totem poles) because of its durability. A huge, fast-growing, shelter-belt tree with looping branches and glossy green leaves which smell of pineapples when crushed. Good for hedges. Avoid shade. 40m (130ft)

T. occidentalis 'Smaragd' – slower growing and forming a narrow column of bright green foliage; good for maintenance-free hedges or towers. Clip the top at the desired height, or leave for a taller, multi-spired effect. 9m (30ft)

T. p. 'Atrovirens - a narrower growing form ideal for dense, uniform hedging. 18m (60ft)

APPENDIX

TWO HORRORS AND A BONUS:
HONEY FUNGUS, BOX BLIGHT AND MYCORRHIZAL FUNGI

HONEY FUNGUS

Every gardener's nightmare, it's an incurable, fatal disease spread by various species of *Armillaria*. They can affect all woody plants, including climbers and some herbaceous perennials, but mainly trees and shrubs. Some species are quite susceptible, others immune. Death can be quick or take years of slow-going, sickly decline (depending on various factors, including the size of the tree), with trees finally succumbing when the infection is at an advanced stage or when stress, for example malnutrition, drought, or water-logging, is the last blow. The healthier the trees are, with good drainage, watering and nutrition, the better their chances of hanging on.

The spread is via root contact between healthy and diseased plants or the tough, leathery, blackish, bootlace-like rhizomorphs travelling (usually) through the top 20cm (8in) of soil; they'll be closer to the surface in heavy, moist soil, and deeper in lighter, drier, well-aerated ones. They grow about 90m (3ft) a year to an astonishing 60m (100ft) or more if they are still attached to a dead tree stump. When they reach a living victim, the bootlaces penetrate the roots; they spread, rot the wood and disrupt the plant's uptake of food and water. Finito. And it's often only then that the cause is discovered. Meanwhile, the rhizomorphs are off again, like a grass snake after a frog.

The first symptoms might well include discoloured leaves, or their non-appearance in spring, with flower buds staying clamped shut before they wither, and shoots dying back, though fruiting/flowering/berrying plants sometimes have one last excellent final fling. Also look out for …

- A white, thin sheet of mushroom-smelling fungal growth or tissue just beneath the bark at the base of the trunk, which must be cut and forced back for inspection.
- Rotting on the woody, badly infected roots.
- Possible bark splitting/leaking gummy resin, again at the base of the tree.
- Possible, weather-dependant clusters of honey-coloured or brownish toadstools with a white ring just below the white gills, in late summer or autumn. They appear around the base of infected plants and dead tree stumps where the fungus can survive, as in the roots, for about 30 years.
- Nearby dying perennials, in which case get them out the ground fast. Find out the cause.

The official remedy in gardens (forget chemicals, they don't apply) is to remove and destroy the entire root system and stump, any adjacent planting (e.g. to 1.2m/4ft either side of an infected plant in a hedge) and the surrounding soil, refilling with "clean" soil. Well, yes, we know, that's OK with perennials and shrubs, but large trees... It's a pain, and means hiring a professional tree surgeon with an excavator or stump grinder.

You can also try creating a vertical barrier against honey fungus attack from a known site using durable, impermeable, heavy gauge plastic sheeting sunk to a maximum depth of 1m (3½ft) in clay, with a 2.5cm (1in) barrier protruding above ground, but that'll probably get the same "Well you do it" response. The good news is that the toadstools can be left, being highly unlikely to cause any problems. It's a matter of aesthetics. (They're said to be edible, but you'll need a metal stomach. Eat them raw or poorly cooked and you'll be running – yodelling - for the loo; possibly even after they're cooked.) The sensible solution is to plant well away from this area, selecting a native tree from the following list. Or move house.

Trees/shrubs currently showing good resistance to honey fungus include:

Buxus (box)

Catalpa

Cercis

Cotinus

Fagus (beech)

Quercus (oak)

Tamarix

Taxus (yew)

Susceptible plants currently include:

Acer (maple)

Araucaria araucana

Betula (birch)

Cedrus (cedar)

Chamaecyparis

Cotoneaster

Crataegus (hawthorn)

x Cupressocyparis leylandii

Cupressus (cypress)

Laburnum

Ligustrum (privet) – a good indicator plant, being one of the first to succumb

Malus (crab apple)

Pinus (but not *P. patula*)

Prunus (ornamental cherry)

Pyracantha

Pyrus (pear)

Salix (willow)

Sequoiadendron giganteum (Wellingtonia/giant redwood)

Ulmus (elm)

Thuja plicata (western red cedar)

BOX BLIGHT

The symptoms of box blight (*Volutella* and *Cylindrocladium*) are brown leaves, defoliation and die-back. Promptly destroy all affected matter (the fungus responsible for *Cylindrocladium* has been known to survive on decomposing leaves for nearly a year, and spores can be spread by human and animal feet to the soil). No fungicides are currently available to amateur gardeners.

Blight can be a nightmare, but some swear by a regular spring feed of seaweed fertilizer that creates strong plants with a good chance of surviving. And when trimming for a smart, compact shape, do so in spring and late summer.

MYCORRHIZAL FUNGI

Mycorrhizal fungi have a positive, symbiotic relationship with plants. They've been working together for millions of years, and a huge percentage of wild plants benefit. The *hyphae* (tubes or strands of fungal tissue) are actually better at taking up water and nutrients than a tree's fine hair roots, and they supply them with extra doses. This extra input can help seedlings put on earlier, stronger growth, and helps trees fight off a variety of problems from drought to soil-borne diseases. In return the plants feed the fungi.

The mycorrhizal fungi can now be quickly applied as a readily available dip (liquid or gel) to the fine roots of bare-root, dormant trees before planting, while containerized plants can be given a granular treatment in the planting hole. Do they really need it? In all gardens with difficult soil and drought, yes, while the fungi provide good health insurance for all containerized plants, being a buffer against the shock of being transplanted. As for established trees, leave them alone. You can try injecting the fungi into the ground, but if the trees have survived this long, why worry?

BIBLIOGRAPHY

If you want the definitive book on all things tree and hedge like, this is NOT it. There's isn't room, even if we wanted to write it. It's an off-beat take on trees and shrubs with ideas for beginners and pros. There are scores of fat, self-satisfied encyclopedias enough which you can't miss, though we'd add a strong caution. Many books are designed first with words filling the tight, empty spaces, and if there's a vital piece of information to go in but no room. That's it. Next subject, next plant. So if you want to know all the ins and out of say, growing box, buy your plants from a specialist box nursery and you'll get more tips in two minutes than from a pile of books that'd you'd be better off Frisbee-ing onto the compost.

This isn't an exhaustive list, but there's enough quality to keep you going.

Alan Mitchell's Trees of Britain, Collins, 1996

The Amazing Book of Mazes, Adrian Fisher, Thames & Hudson, 2006

Arborsculpture, Richard Reames, Arborsmith Studios, 2005
    Website: **www.arborsmith.com**

Architectural Plants, Christine Shaw, Collins, 2005

Architectural Plants, catalogue. Address: Nuthurst, Horsham, West Sussex RH13 6LH.
    Email: **www.architecturalplants.com**

Bark, Ghillean Tolmie Prance and Anne E. Prance, Timber Press, 1993

Cassell's Trees of Britain & and Northern Ireland, David More and John White, Cassell, 2003

Champion Trees of Britain and Ireland, Owen Johnson, Whittet Books, 2003

Classic Garden Design, Rosemary Verey, Viking, 1984

The Chinese Garden, Maggie Keswick, Frances Lincoln, revised edition 2003

Creating a Chinese Garden, David Engel, Croom Helm, 1986

Creating Small Formal Gardens, Roy Strong, Conran Octopus, 1989

Creating Period Gardens, Elizabeth Banks, Phaidon, 1991

Fantastic Trees, Edwin A. Messinger, Timber Press, 1999

Flowering Plants of the World, ed. V. H. Heywood, Oxford UniversityPress, 1978

The Garden Tree, Alan Mitchell and Allen Coombes, Weidenfeld and Nicolson, 1998

Garden Trees (Garden Guide), Richard Rosenfeld, Dorling Kindersley, 2004

Gardens in China, Peter Valder, Timber Press, 2002

The Great Hedge of India, Roy Moxham, Constable, 2001

The Heritage Trees of Britain & Northern Ireland, Jon Stokes and Donald Roger, Constable, 2004

The Hillier Manual of Trees & Shrubs, David & Charles, 2004

The History of the Countryside, Oliver Rackham, Dent, 1986

Japanese Garden Design, Marc Peter Keane, Tuttle Publishing, 1996

Japanese Gardens For Today, David Engel, Tuttle Publishing, 1959

Knot Gardens and Parterres, Robin Whalley and Anne Jennings, Barn Elms, 1998

Landscape and Memory, Simon Schama, HarperCollins, 1995

The Last Forest, Oliver Rackham, Dent, 1989

The Medieval Garden, Sylvia Landsberg, British Museum Press, 1995

Mediaeval Gardens, John Harvey, Batsford, 1981

Meetings With Remarkable Trees, Thomas Pakenham, Weidenfeld and Nicolson, 1996

The Nature of Mediterranean Europe: An Ecological History, A. T. Grove and Oliver Rackham, Yale, 2001

Recreating The Period Garden, Edited by Graham Stuart Thomas, The National Trust, 1984

Remarkable Trees of the World, Thomas Pakenham, Weidenfeld and Nicolson, 2002

The Renaissance Garden in England, Roy Strong, Thames & Hudson, 1979

RHS Plant Finder, Dorling Kindersley, annually updated

The Royal Horticultural Society Pruning & Training, C. Brickell and D. Joyce, Dorling Kindersley, 1996

Scholar Gardens of China, Stewart R. Johnston, Cambridge University Press, 1991

The Secret Life of Trees, Colin Tudge, Allen Lane, 2005

Secret Teachings in the Art of Japanese Gardens, David Lawson, Kodansha, 1987

Topiary, A. M. Clevely, HarperCollins, 1988

Topiary, David Joyce, Frances Lincoln, 1999

Tree Bark, A Colour Guide, Hugues Vaucher, Timber Press, 2003

Treehouses, Paula Henderson and Adam Mornement, Frances Lincoln, 2005

Trees, Roland Ennos, The Natural History Museum, 2001

Trees and Shrubs Hardy in the British Isles, W. J. Bean, John Murray, 1991

Trees & Woodland in the British Landscape, Oliver Rackham, Dent, revised 1993

The Trees That Made Britain, Archie Miles, BBC Books, 2006

Trees, Woodlands and Western Civilization, Richard Hayman, Hambledon & London, 2003

The Well Furnished Garden, Michael Balston, Mitchell Beazley, 1990

The Wildwood, Gareth Lovett Hones and Richard Mabey, Aurum Press, 1993

Woodlands, Oliver Rackham, HarperCollins, 2006

INDEX

TREE TRICKS INDEX

PICTURE ACKNOWLEDGEMENTS

All photography is by Jo Whitworth, unless credited below. The publishers would like to thank the following sources for their kind permission to reproduce the photographs and illustrations in this book. Our best efforts were made to locate the copyright owners. We apologise in advance for any unintentional omission and will be pleased to insert the appropriate acknowledgement in subsequent editions of this work.

Key
BAL = Bridgeman Art Library
Richard Reames = Richard Reames, author *Arborsculpture – Solutions for a Small Planet,* www.arborsmith.com

2 Ivan Hicks, 6 Photolibrary Group/Juliet Greene/Tom Stuart-Smith, 10-11 Andrew Lawson, 14 Tibor Bognár/Corbis, 16 Ivan Hicks, 22-23 Jerry Harpur/StanHywett, 28r Andrew Lawson/Burr Castle, Ireland, 31 Andrew Lawson/Julie Toll, 35 Record Trees, 36 Marianne Majerus/IvanHicks, 44 Ivan Hicks, 50-51 Edward Parker/Alamy, 54 Andrew Lawson/Coton Manor, Northants, 57 Marianne Majerus, 59 Marianne Majerus/Susan Campbell, 65 Aharon Naveh, 66l Ed Webber/Covello & Covello (courtesy Richard Reames) 67r Richard Reames, 72l Andrew Lawson/Old Rectory, Sudborough, 77 Andrew Lawson, 78 Ivan Hicks, 81 Ivan Hicks, 82r Ivan Hicks, 83 Kent Klich/MIRA, 88l Jerry Harpur/Hatfield House, 91 Rob Whitworth/Designer: Henk Gerritson, Priona Gardens, Netherlands, 93 Photolibrary Group/Howard Rice, 95t Andrew Lawson, 95b Mariannne Majerus/Lynne Marcus & John Hall/Gardens & Beyond, 104 Private Collection, The Stapleton Collection/BAL, 105 Jonathan Buckley, 106 Marianne Majerus/Alain Provost, 107 Andrew Lawson/Arabella Lennox-Boyd, 108 Jerry Harpur/Jardins du Prieure Notre Dame d'Orsan, France, 109 Marianne Majerus/Jessica Duncan, 111 Andrew Lawson/Docton Mill, Devon, 114-115 Jody Boyman, 116 Musee Marmottan, Paris, France/BAL, 119 courtesy of Richard Reames, 121t Richard Reames, 121b Freedom Lohr, 122 Wilma Erlandson Collection (courtesy of Richard Reames), 125 Richard Reames

Additional credits for Jo Whitworth photography.
Garden designer: Ivan Hicks, unless credited below:
5 Marchants Hardy Plants Nursery, Laughton, E. Sussex, 29 Designer Anita Pereire, 37 Broughton Grange, 87 Wat Phra Kaeo Temple, Bangkok, Thailand, 102-3 Wyken Hall, Suffolk, 138 RHS Gardens, Wisley